THE ECONOMIC CRISIS AND THE STATE OF ECONOMICS

THE ECONOMIC CRISIS AND THE STATE OF ECONOMICS

Edited by Robert Skidelsky and Christian Westerlind Wigström

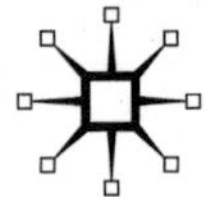

THE ECONOMIC CRISIS AND THE STATE OF ECONOMICS
Copyright © Robert Skidelsky and Christian Westerlind Wigström, 2010.

First published in 2010 by
PALGRAVE MACMILLAN®
in the United States—a division of St. Martin's Press LLC,
175 Fifth Avenue, New York, NY 10010.

Where this book is distributed in the UK, Europe and the rest of the world,
this is by Palgrave Macmillan, a division of Macmillan Publishers Limited,
registered in England, company number 785998, of Houndmills,
Basingstoke, Hampshire RG21 6XS.

Palgrave Macmillan is the global academic imprint of the above companies
and has companies and representatives throughout the world.

Palgrave® and Macmillan® are registered trademarks in the United States,
the United Kingdom, Europe and other countries.

ISBN: 978–0–230–10254–5

Library of Congress Cataloging-in-Publication Data

The economic crisis and the state of economics / edited by Robert
Skidelsky and Christian Westerlind Wigstrom.
   p. cm.
Includes index.
ISBN 978–0–230–10254–5
1. Global Financial Crisis, 2008–2009. 2. Economic history—
21st century. 3. Economics. 4. Recessions. I. Skidelsky, Robert Jacob
Alexander, 1939– II. Wigstrom, Christian Westerlind.

HB37172008–2009 .E36 2010
330.9—dc22   2009040062

A catalogue record of the book is available from the British Library.

Design by Newgen Imaging Systems (P) Ltd., Chennai, India.

First edition: March 2010

10 9 8 7 6 5 4 3 2 1

Printed in the United States of America.

To economists, who may some day apply common sense.

CONTENTS

PREFACE

Robert Skidelsky

This book is the product of a symposium that I hosted on February 13, 2009. It was partly inspired by a dissatisfaction with the silence of the economics profession on the causes of and the remedies for the current economic downturn. Here was an event that was freely being compared to the Great Depression but comments in the financial press were being provided entirely by financial journalists. Where were the economists? Here are some of the best of the economists and they do indeed have something to say. A second inspiration for the symposium was that the present crisis has brought to a head a moral dissatisfaction with the quality of capitalist civilization—obsession with growth at all costs, neglect of traditional social values, and a lack of concern for the environment. Many of these criticisms emerged as an attack on globalization, but they have been given added point by the current crisis. Today we have the attacks on "obscene" executive bonuses and the sense of decline of social responsibility. These are moral critiques, and I thought it would be interesting to ask questions not just about the moral critique as it applies to the economic situation, but also as it applies to the economics profession's understanding of moral issues.

I would like to thank Pavel Erochkine, Louis Mosley, Chelsea Renton, and Christian Westerlind Wigström for their help in organizing the conference, and the House of Lords for providing facilities for holding it. In editing the papers for publication I have abandoned any attempt to make them all equally intelligible to non-economists. Much of economics is technically difficult, requiring some knowledge of mathematics and statistics. Most of it is more opaque than it needs to be because economists, like other social scientists, speak to each other in a kind of short-hand which defies outside understanding. But the courageous reader will catch a flavor of the argument even in the few technical essays in this collection.

Essays by:

Christopher Bliss, Richard Bronk, Paul Davidson, Meghnad Desai, Charles Goodhart, Vijay Joshi, John Kay, Sujoy Mukerji, Marc Potters, and Edward Skidelsky

Contributions to the discussion from:

John Aisbitt, Gerald Holtham, Geoffrey Hosking, Will Hutton, Paul Klemperer, Richard Layard, Peter Lilley, and Bill Robinson

ABOUT THE CONTRIBUTORS

Christopher Bliss
Professorial Fellow and Nuffield Professor of International Economics 1976–2007, University of Oxford. Author of *Trade, Growth and Inequality* (2007).

Richard Bronk
Visiting Fellow, London School of Economics. Author of *The Romantic Economist: Imagination in Economics* (2009).

Paul Davidson
Emeritus Professor of Economics, University of Tennessee. Editor of the *Journal of Post Keynesian Economics* and member of the Editorial Board of *Ekonomia*. He is the author, co-author, or editor of twenty-two books, the most recent one being *The Keynes Solution* (2009).

Meghnad Desai
Emeritus Professor of Economics, London School of Economics, and member of the House of Lords. Author of *Marx's Revenge: The Resurgence of Capitalism and the Death of Statist Socialism* (2002) and *Nehru's Hero: Dilip Kumar in the Life of India* (2004).

Charles Goodhart
Emeritus Professor of Banking and Finance, London School of Economics. Former member of the MPC. Former advisor to the Governor of the Bank of England.

Vijay Joshi

Fellow of St John's College, and Emeritus Fellow of Merton College, Oxford. Co-author of *India: Macroeconomics and Political Economy* (1994). Former Economic Advisor to the Government of India and the World Bank.

John Kay

Visiting Professor, London School of Economics, and weekly columnist in the *Financial Times*. Author of *The Long and the Short of It* (2009).

Sujoy Mukerji

Professor of Economics, University of Oxford, and the author of articles on uncertainty and ambiguity.

Marc Potters

Head of Research at Capital Fund Management, and co-author of *Theory of Financial Risk and Derivative Pricing* (2003).

Edward Skidelsky

Lecturer in Philosophy, University of Exeter, and author of *Ernst Cassirer: The Last Philosopher of Culture* (2009).

Robert Skidelsky

Emeritus Professor of Political Economy, University of Warwick, and member of the House of Lords. Author of a three-volume biography of John Maynard Keynes and *Keynes: The Return of the Master* (2009).

Christian Westerlind Wigström

PhD student in International Relations at the University of Oxford.

ABOUT THE DISCUSSANTS

John Aisbitt
Chairman of the Man Group plc and former partner at Goldman Sachs.

Gerald Holtham
Managing Partner of Cadwyn Capital LLP and Visiting Professor at Cardiff Business School. He was formerly Chief International Economist at Lehman Brothers, Europe, and Head of the General Economics Division at the OECD in Paris.

Geoffrey Hosking
Emeritus Professor Russian History, University College London.

Will Hutton
Executive Vice-Chair of The Work Foundation, weekly columnist, and the author of *The Writing On The Wall: China and the West in the 21st Century* (2007). He is a former editor-in-chief of *The Observer*.

Paul Klemperer
Edgeworth Professor of Economics, University of Oxford, and author of *Auctions: Theory and Practice* (2004).

Richard Layard
Programme Director at the Centre for Economic Performance, London School of Economics, and member of the House of Lords. He is the author of *Happiness: Lessons from a New Science* (2005).

Peter Lilley

MP since 1983, former Secretary of State for Trade and Industry 1990–1992, Secretary of State for Social Security 1992–1997 and Shadow Chancellor of the Exchequer 1997–1998.

Bill Robinson

Chief Economist at KPMG, former Head UK Business Economist at PricewaterhouseCoopers.

THE ECONOMIC CRISIS AND THE STATE OF ECONOMICS

INTRODUCTION

Robert Skidelsky and Christian Westerlind Wigström

K eynes wrote of his *General Theory of Employment, Interest, and Money* (1936) that it was "an attempt to bring to an issue deep divergences of opinion between fellow economists which has for the time being destroyed the practical influence of economic theory." That seems not unlike the situation at the moment. A heated discussion between rival schools has been going on in the blogosphere; of this, hardly an echo appears even in the financial press. The foremost battle concerns the effects of the "stimulus." This is waged between the "freshwater economists" of Chicago University and the "saltwater economists" of the east and west coasts. Eugene Fama, who is a Professor of Finance at Chicago University, and the godfather of the Efficient Market Theory, encapsulated the Chicago view when he said that all a stimulus did was to shift resources from the private to the public sector of the economy, so that its stimulating effect was, in effect, zero, or even less. An enraged Paul Krugman responded that this was to take economics back to the dark ages. The historically minded will recall that this is a re-run of the debates about policies for the Great Depression. Keynes wrote his *General Theory* to refute the "Treasury View" of the 1920s that the only effect of public spending was to "crowd out" private spending.

Keynes argued this was true only if the economy was fully employed. If there were unemployed resources, extra public spending could take the place of the absent private spending, and thus raise aggregate demand to a full employment level. Underlying this debate is a basic disagreement between economists about how the economy works. If you believe that it is always fully employed, or that recessions are in some sense "optimal," then it follows that a "stimulus" will do no good. If you believe, with Keynes, that collapses of aggregate spending are possible, then a "stimulus" can improve the situation. The fact that this kind of debate is interminable only shows how far economics is from being the natural science many of its practitioners claim it to be.

Papers and Discussion

Three main themes emerged from the papers and the discussions that followed: the question of whether future events are a matter of uncertainty rather than risk; the impact of global macroeconomic imbalances; and the role of economic models. Paul Davidson strongly advocates a view of the future as irreducibly uncertain. Unlike in the "hard sciences" such as physics or astronomy, in economics, there is no foundation on which to base any probabilities about future events. While astronomers can be reasonably confident that a planet will appear in a predicted place at a predicted time the same cannot be said about many subjects of interest to economists. Probabilities calculated on past and current market data cannot be taken to hold about future events since, as Davidson argues, there is no way of knowing what social and economic events will occur in the future. Thus, the future is not "ergodic"—it is not predetermined. Yet, the ergodic axiom is at the heart of key theories such as the efficient-market hypothesis which states that markets price assets correctly based on all available past and present information. Without the possibility of assigning actuarial probabilities to future events, the value of assets cannot be efficiently established. In effect, the efficient-market hypothesis assumes that all uncertainty can be reduced to calculable risk. The failure to recognize this fallacy has led to the bankruptcy of major financial institutions such as AIG as well as a false sense of security which paved the way for panic once the foundations trembled. Davidson argues for the introduction of a "market maker"—an institution that assumes responsibility for keeping the market liquid in the face of unforeseeable events—in order to lessen the effects of uncertainty. Sujoy Mukerji lends support to Davidson's emphasis on irreducible uncertainty as an explanation for the crisis. In situations of uncertainty it is often the case that the decision maker's knowledge about the likelihood of contingent events is consistent with more than one probability. Under such conditions it is rational not to act. In financial markets this leads to a situation in which more ambiguity results in less trade and lending. "The uncertainty is triggered by unusual events and untested financial innovations that lead agents to question their worldview." In other words, rather than subjecting investments to incalculable risks no investments are made at all. Instead, people hoard cash—an idea conforming to Keynes's liquidity preference theory. Thus, the present crisis can be understood as having erupted because of increasing uncertainty amidst rapid financial innovation—an idea closely related to the discussion in Richard Bronk's chapter. At some point investors and banks withdrew their capital and credit, leaving consumers and companies and ultimately themselves without adequate financing. This suggests that a policy promoting transparency and other uncertainty-reducing objectives could mitigate the financial downturn and ease credit markets. We are in need of qualitative rather than quantitative easing. Marc Potters, on the other hand, does not dismiss the ability of economic modeling to assign accurately probabilities to future events. The future is not exclusively characterized by irreducible uncertainty. During the discussion this position was seconded by Paul Klemperer. Christopher Bliss who supported this stand went on to say that if the past and present say nothing about the future, as Davidson's rejection of the ergodic axiom implies, "We might as well all go home." Potters argues that, rather than facing a *principal* problem with uncertainty, influential pricing models have typically relied on assumptions too simple to have any relation to the reality they seek to predict. For instance, the Gaussian processes assumed in the Black and Scholes option pricing model imply a disregard for the relative frequency of extreme fluctuations observed in the empirical data. In contrast to the assumptions of this model, volatility is not constant. The invalidity of these assumptions implies that there can be no zero-risk options as the model predicts. In other words, "option trading involves some irreducible risk." Moreover, conventional wisdom in mathematical finance treats prices as "god-given," yet feedback loops indicate that this is fundamentally wrong. Large purchases of assets increase their price thereby prompting further purchases, or—conversely—decreasing prices result in investors selling thereby further lowering the price. In effect, the financial crisis can be explained by means of such a positive feedback loop. Under such circumstances the degree of correlation among instruments changes—a consideration only very rarely included in financial mathematical models. Mathematical tractability and methodological consistency have made these models attractive, despite their flaws. However, if the models were better understood and improved there is scope for modeling to reduce the degree of uncertainty in the economy. The problem is that a lot of people can make huge amounts of money by *not* understanding the models they are using. This ties in with Christopher Bliss's emphasis on asymmetric information: bankers provide credit to investment projects they have only very limited information about. Rating agencies and diversification of asset portfolios are intended to reduce the risk associated with asymmetric information, yet the rating agencies have incentives to award higher ratings than deserved and, as Potters points out, diversified portfolios do not reduce risk as soon price movements are correlated. Thus, according to Bliss, "markets function poorly, if they function at all, in situations characterized by asymmetric information." And this problem is exacerbated when the distinction between investment and retail banks is blurred. "Safe" deposits end up being used for speculation. Once the bubble bursts the crisis migrates quickly from finance to the real economy. However, asymmetric information only explains the speculative side of the crisis—it does not explain how consumers in the West could enjoy low inflation, cheap money and high profits at the same time—all of which fuelled an unprecedented growth in credit.

Bliss argues that competition from East Asia, predominantly China, was responsible for this. A Chinese "saving glut" in the form of enormous investments in American Treasury Bills kept the Chinese currency artificially low and made Chinese companies super competitive. Cheap imports kept prices low while cheap Chinese labor stifled the increase in Western real wages. In effect, the resulting imbalances led to a situation in which East Asia financed Western current account deficits. Vijay Joshi explains the origins of the Asian saving glut by referring to two projects: the creation of foreign currency reserves as a precautionary buffer—the value of which the East Asian countries understood after the 1997 financial crisis; and the policy decision of these states to pursue export-led growth as a means to economic development. Both projects were facilitated by keeping their own currencies low relative to the reserve currency—the dollar. This was achieved by investing heavily in the American credit markets. The ensuing macroeconomic imbalances were not sustainable in the long run. Joshi argues that had American house prices not fallen, an adjustment process would have started with a fall of the dollar. The question of why central banks don't prick bubbles before they become unmanageable was raised in the discussion with Peter Lilley pointing to the political consequences of halting growth at a time when it is difficult to establish whether the economy truly is experiencing a bubble or not. Joshi argued that in order to forestall similar bubbles appearing in the future central banks on a national level, must look beyond consumer price indices as key indicators of the health of the economy. They need to look at asset and credit price movements too. Bill Robinson agreed with the view that central banks require further tools along side the interest rate: for example, a mandate to regulate banks' capital charges. Joshi called for a strengthening of key financial institutions such as the IMF to prevent the creation of unsustainable imbalances on an international level. The world needs a "neutral" reserve currency and agreements on exchange rate regimes. Although macroeconomic theory cannot be blamed for global imbalances, it shows weakness in its inability to foresee these consequences. In part this weakness stems from reliance on inappropriate models—a theme strongly represented both in the papers and discussions. To John Kay "the test of an economic model is whether it is useful rather than whether it is true." We should not be concerned about whether the efficient-market theory is true or not. It is neither. Markets are often efficient but economists take this to mean that they are always efficient. Information is included in prices but it is not necessarily correctly weighted. The same goes for views on risk. The theory of subjective expected utility is neither true nor false. It is illuminating. Economic theories are metaphors and models and not realistic descriptions. We need to be able to choose when to use which metaphor. "The skill of the economist is in deciding which of many incommensurable models one should apply in a particular context." Keynesian uncertainty which considers confidence, narratives and degrees of belief in those narratives has all but become extinct yet Keynes's perception of risk is no less important than the dominant classical risk paradigm. Economists need to be eclectic. Otherwise we end up in the situation described by Charles Goodhart. Goodhart describes how Dynamic Stochastic General Equilibrium (DSGE) models work well in good times when default rates on loans are low but badly in bad times. In part he attributes this weakness to the transversality condition which stipulates that an economic agent has used all his resources and paid all his debts by the time he dies. This, Goodhart observes, hardly corresponds to reality. Amongst economists a flawed but rigorous theory often beats a correct but literary exposition. This has led to an overconfidence in markets based on rigorous but incorrect theories such as the efficient market theory. However, there is a large difference between what academic economists think and what businessmen do. Given that economists and financial practitioners accept that prices can move away from fundamentals it is absurd to believe in the efficient market theory. Consequently, "our standard macro models [...], which virtually everybody has been using, tell us absolutely nothing about our present problems." This mismatch between how economists and the business world interpret data is the starting point for Richard Bronk's paper. Despite rapid innovation having introduced dynamism and uncertainty, economists rely on equilibrium models and risk. This is, Bronk argues, a result of the choice of metaphors employed within economics and thereby links up with Kay's view of economic models as illuminations rather than descriptions of reality. In the discussion, Paul Klemperer agreed with this: models are metaphors, often with multiple interpretations. Different settings, Klemperer argued, requires different models often based on an understanding of sociology and psychology. According to Bronk the Romantics looked at the nature of creativity and concluded that the world as we see it is, to some extent, a creation of our minds. The way we use models structures the way we analyze and interpret what we observe. "If the model seems to be useful, you may soon forget how necessarily stylized this picture is." Your perspective affects your view. Newtonian analogies suggest equilibria where romanticism would have pointed to dynamism. No one model says everything. Contemporary models' tendency to treat uncertainty as risk has had huge consequences for the world economy and contributed to the crisis, as Davidson and Mukerji noted. Bronk notes that "there was, in retrospect, something absurd in relying so completely on risk models based on correlations trawled from data on the past at the very moment when bankers were creating new complex products each and every week." Again, this points not only to the necessity of greater care when choosing models but also to the need for a greater awareness of the biases that come with it. Meghnad Desai's chapter illustrates the point. The streamlining of economic theory has limited the realm of possible approaches to analyzing and mitigating the current crisis by excluding certain perspectives. He argues that we should look at the ideas developed by Hayek to get a better idea of the unfolding of recent events. Hayek combined Walras with money to explain business cycles. Credit creation by the banking system produces overinvestment in relation to voluntary saving. The overinvestment can be kept going only by injecting more and more inflation into the system. In raising the rate of interest to liquidate inflation banks curtail the credit needed to complete the investment projects so investment collapses, and the economy contracts. Hayek believed that once the credit creation had occurred there was no way of mitigating the subsequent collapse. The important thing was to prevent the excessive credit creation in the first place. Hayek has long disappeared from economic textbooks yet, as Desai remarks, "if you cast your memory back, economics was never uniform." A heterogeneous discipline is needed once again. Edward Skidelsky argues that the moral underpinnings of the discipline have to be enriched as well. Whereas classical economics was concerned with agents acting in pure self-interest, today's economics is—though based on choices between competing preferences—silent as to the content of those preferences. The absence of preference content can be seen as a sign of tolerance. However, Skidelsky argues that egoism remains implicit in the method of economics. Economists do not tackle the non-economic side of life yet aspire to explain everything. Although not all goods are commensurable, economists treat them as subject to equal trades. A moral person does not weigh the costs and benefits of stealing a wallet. He does what he knows is right. The moral principle cannot be traded against the bank balance. Simplification deprives economics of the power to tackle many of the problems it seeks to solve. Reflecting Bliss's remark that "insecurity and inequality are what matter most" in terms of making people unhappy—not absolute income and growth—Skidelsky highlights the importance of non-economic considerations which economics ignores. It goes without saying, that a single day's discussion could not cover all the issues raised by the title of this symposium. One of the most fruitful results was the widespread agreement on the need for a "horses for courses" approach to economic modeling. This corresponds to Keynes's view that we need different economic models for different states of the world. It is useless to try to construct a tight, mathematical model that is supposed to be universally valid. The beauty of his own *General Theory of Employment, Interest, and Money* was that it was "general" enough to accommodate a variety of "models" applicable to different states of expectations. According to this theory, markets could behave in ways described by the classical and new classical theories, but they need not, and probably usually did not. So it was important to take precautions against bad behavior. The key problem, as Keynes pointed out, was the difficulty of deciding which model applies to which conditions. He wrote:

> Economics is a science of thinking in terms of models jointed to the art of choosing models which are relevant to the contemporary world. It is compelled to be this, because, unlike the typical natural science, the material to which it is applied is, in too many respects, not homogeneous through time.... Good economists are scarce because the gift of using "vigilant observation" to choose good models, although it does not require a highly specialised intellectual technique, appears to be a very rare one. JMK, *Collected Writings*, Volume 14, pp. 296–297

PART I

RISK AND UNCERTAINTY IN ECONOMICS

CHAPTER 1

RISK AND UNCERTAINTY

Paul Davidson

Politicians and talking heads on television are continuously reminding the public that the current economic crisis that began in 2007 as a small sub prime mortgage default problem in the United States has created the greatest economic catastrophe since the Great Depression. As I pointed out in two recent articles (Davidson, 2008a,[1] Davidson 2008b,[2]) it is the deregulation of the financial system that began in the 1970s in the United States that is the basic cause of our current financial market distress. Yet for more than three decades, mainstream academic economists, policymakers in government, central bankers, and their economic advisors insisted that (1) government regulations of markets and large government spending policies are the cause of our economic problems and (2) consequently, the solution to our economic problems is to end big government and freeing markets from government regulatory controls In an amazing "mea culpa" testimony before Congress on October 23, 2008, Alan Greenspan, the former chairman of the Federal Reserve of the United States, admitted that he had overestimated the ability of free financial markets to self-correct and he had entirely missed the possibility that deregulation could unleash such a destructive force on the economy. Greenspan stated:

> This crisis, however, has turned out to be much broader than any-
> thing I could have imagined.... those of us who had looked to the
> self-interest of lending institutions to protect shareholder's equity
> (myself especially) are in a state of shocked disbelief....In recent
> decades, a vast risk management and pricing system has evolved,
> combining the best insights of mathematicians and finance experts
> supported by major advances in computer and communications
> technology. A Nobel Prize [in economics] was awarded for the dis-
> covery of the [free market] pricing model that underpins much of
> the advance in [financial] derivatives markets. This modern risk
> management paradigm held sway for decades. The whole intellec-
> tual edifice, however, [has] collapsed.

Under questioning by members of the Congressional committee
Greenspan admitted: "I found a flaw in the model that I perceive
is the critical functioning structure that defines how the world
works. That's precisely the reason I was shocked....I still do not
fully understand why it happened, and obviously to the extent that
I figure it happened and why, I shall change my views." The purpose of this chapter is to explain to Greenspan and others who
believed that the solutions to our economic problems are free efficient markets why they are wrong.

Theories Explaining the Operation of a Capitalist Economy

There are two fundamental economic theories that attempt to
explain the operation of a capitalist economy: (1) The classical economic theory which is sometimes referred to as "the theory of
efficient markets" or mainstream economic theory." The mantra
of this analytical system is that free markets can cure any economic
problem that may arise, while government interference always
causes economic problems. In other words, government economic
policy is the problem, the free market is the solution. (2) Keynes's
liquidity theory of an entrepreneurial economy.

The conclusions of this analysis is that government can cure, with cooperation of private industry and households, economic flaws inherent in the operation of a capitalist economy where unfettered greed and fear are permitted to dominate economic decisions. Time is a device for preventing everything from happening at once. Economic decisions made today will have outcomes that can only be evaluated days, months or even years in the future. The basic—but not the only—difference between these two theories is how they treat knowledge about future outcomes of present decisions. In essence, the classical theory presumes that by one method or another, decision makers today can, and do, possess knowledge about the future. Thus the only economic problem that markets have to solve is the allocation of resources to meet the most valuable outcomes of current and future dates. The Keynes liquidity theory, on the other hand, presumes that decision makers "know" that they do not, and cannot, know the future outcome of certain crucial economic decisions made today. Thus Keynes theory explains how the capitalist economic system creates institutions that permit decision makers to deal with an uncertain future while making allocative decisions and then sleep well at night.

Reading Tea Leaves: The Classical Solution for Knowing the Future

Advocates of classical economics believe that free markets are efficient. In a classical efficient market it is presumed that there are large numbers of rational decision makers who, before making a purchase or sales decision, collect and analyze reliable information which is available to all on both the probability of events that have already occurred and on the probability of events that will occur in the future. In previous centuries, economists such as Adam Smith and David Ricardo merely assumed that today's market participants possessed complete information about the future and that these participants would always make correct decisions that represented their own best interests. To some an assumption that the future is already known may seem preposterous. Nevertheless, this idea underlies Greenspan's belief (cited above) that the self-interest of lending institutions in a free market led management to undertake transactions that protected shareholder's equity. The classical presumption that the future is known is the foundation of all of today's efficient market theories. For example, the mathematically sophisticated Arrow–Debreu general equilibrium model is the basic analytical framework upon which most mathematical computer models used by economists are based.

The Arrow–Debreu presumption is that markets exist today to permit participants to buy and sell at any given time now or later. Thus at the initial instant of time, it is presumed that all market participants enter into transactions for the purchases and sales of all products and services deliverable not only in the present but also in the future till the end of time. In its extreme conceptualization, this complex mathematical model implies that buyers today not only know what goods and services they are going to demand in the market today, tomorrow, and every future date for the rest of their lives, but also "know" what their grandchildren and great-grandchildren will want to buy and sell decades and centuries from now. Had efficient markets existed since the beginning of time, then Adam and Eve, being ancestors to all of us alive today, would already have entered a future order to purchase tomorrow's London theater tickets for me. Only the high level of mathematics and abstraction of this classical theory can bury its impossible axiomatic foundation. Many of today's mainstream classical economists, however, recognize that the Arrow–Debreu presumption of the existence of a complete set of markets for every conceivable good and service for every future date till the end of time is impossible. Nevertheless they still believe in the efficiency of free markets. To salvage their efficient market conclusions, they assume that market participants possess "rational expectations" regarding all future possible outcomes of any decision made today. Lucas's theory of rational expectations asserts that though individuals presumably make decisions based on their subjective probability distributions, if expectations are to be rational these subjective distributions must be equal to the objective probability distributions that will govern outcomes at any particular future date. In other words, today's rational market participants somehow possess statistically reliable information regarding the probability distribution of the universe of future events of any specific future date. From a technical point of view, in order to obtain a reliable probability distribution about a future universe, the analyst should draw a random sample from that future universe. Then market participants can analyze this sample to calculate statistically reliable information about the mean, standard deviation, etc. of this future population. Thus, the analyst can reduce uncertainty about prospective outcomes to a future of actuarial certainties expressed as objective probabilistic risks. Since drawing a sample from the future is not possible, efficient market theorists must presume that probabilities calculated from already existing market data are equivalent to drawing a sample from markets that will exist in the future. This presumption is known as the ergodic axiom that in essence presumes that the future is merely the statistical shadow of the past. Only if this ergodic axiom is accepted as a universal truth, will calculating probability distributions (risks) on the basis of historical market data be statistically equivalent to drawing and analyzing samples from the future. Those who claim that economics is a "hard science" like physics or astronomy argue that the ergodic assumption must be the foundation of the economists' model. In 1969, for example, Nobel Prize economist Paul Samuelson,[3] who is often thought to be the originator of post–Second World War "Keynesianism," wrote that if economists hope to remove economics from the realm of history and move it into the "realm of science" we must impose what Samuelson called the "ergodic hypothesis." The highly complex computer models used by investment bankers on Wall Street in recent years to evaluate and manage the risks of dealings with financial assets are based on statistical probability analysis of historical data to predict the future. Given the necessity of the government to bail out all these Wall Street investment bankers when their risk management tools failed, it should be obvious that their risk management computer models presumed the ergodic axiom while the real world is nonergodic. This is why all these risk management models failed to predict the 2008 future. (Hopefully Alan Greenspan will now understand why his ergodic axiom based intellectual edifice failed.)

An axiom is defined as a universal truth that needs not be proved. The classical ergodic axiom permits economists to claim that probabilities calculated from past and current market data provide reliable actuarial knowledge about the future. In other words, the future is merely probabilistically risky but not uncertain and that the future path of the economy is predetermined and cannot be changed by human action today.

Astronomers insist that the future path of the planets around the sun and that of the moon around the earth has been predetermined since the moment of the Big Bang beginning of the universe. Nothing that humans do can change the predetermined path of these heavenly bodies. This Big Bang theory means that the "hard science" of astronomy relies on the ergodic axiom. Consequently, by using past measurements of the speed and direction of celestial objects, astronomical scientists can accurately predict the time (usually within seconds) of the next solar eclipse. The ergodic nature of astronomy is given and proven, so it should be obvious that the U.S. Congress cannot pass legislation that will actually prevent future solar eclipses from occurring even if the legislation is designed to obtain more sunshine to improve agriculture crop production. In a similar vein, if, as Samuelson claims, economics is a "hard science" based on the ergodic axiom, then Congress cannot pass a law preventing the next economic problem from occurring anymore than it can prevent the next eclipse. Efficient market theorists, who believe they profess a hard science, therefore must argue that Congress cannot pass legislations that permanently alter the predetermined future path of the economy. At most, logically consistent efficient market analysis indicates that active government policies that interfere with free markets deliver an "external shock" to the system which will, at most, push the economy off from its projected future efficient path into a path of unemployment, resource waste, and even inflation. If, however, markets are free and efficient, then actions by rational market participants will restore, in some unspecified time (i.e., the long run), the system back to its predetermined efficient path by purging "the rottenness out of the system" (to use Secretary of Treasury Andrew Mellon's elegant admonition to President Hoover whenever the latter wanted to take positive action to end the Great Depression). The Oxford mathematician Jerome Ravitz in an article entitled "Faith and Reason in The Mathematics of the Credit Crunch" appearing in *Oxford Magazine* (eighth week, Michaelmas term, 2008) has written:

> Mathematics first provided an enabling technology with computers, then with a plausible theorem it offered legitimation for runaway speculation....it framed the quantitative specification of its fantasized products. Mathematics thereby became uniquely toxic, what Warren Buffet has called "weapons of mass destruction."

If Keynes were alive today I think he might have called today's theory of efficient markets a case of "weapons of math destruction." Yet, economist Robert Lucas admits that the axioms underlying classical economics are "artificial, abstract, patently unreal."[4] Despite this, Lucas, like, Samuelson, insists such unreal assumptions are the only scientific method of doing economics. Lucas insists that "progress in economic thinking means getting better and better abstract, analogue models, not better verbal observations about the real world."[5] In the introduction to his book *Against the Gods* (John Wiley, 1998)—a treatise that deals with the questions of relevance of risk management techniques on Wall Street—Peter L. Bernstein writes:

> The story that I have to tell is marked all the way through by a persistent tension between those who assert that the best decisions are based on quantification and numbers, determined by the [statistical] patterns of the past, and those who based their decisions on a more subjective degree of belief about the uncertain future. This is a controversy that has never been resolved. One would hope that the empirical evidence of the collapse of those "masters of the economic universe" that have dominated Wall Street machinations for the past three decades has at least created doubt regarding the applicability of classical ergodic theory to our economic world.

Keynes's Liquidity Theory for Dealing with the Uncertain Future

John Maynard Keynes's ideas support Bernstein's latter group. Keynes specifically argued that the uncertainty of the economic future cannot be resolved by looking at statistical patterns of the past. Keynes believed that today's economic decisions of individuals regarding spending and saving depend on their subjective beliefs regarding possible future events. Keynes thought that classical economists "resemble Euclidean Geometers in a non-Euclidean world who, discovering that in experience straight lines apparently parallel often meet, rebuke the lines for not keeping straight—as the only remedy for the unfortunate collisions which are occurring. Yet in truth there is no remedy except to throw over the axiom of parallels and to work out a non-Euclidean geometry. Something similar is required today in economics."[6] To create non-Euclidean economics to explain why these unemployment "collisions" occur in the world of experience Keynes had to deny ("throw over") the relevance of several classical axioms for understanding the real world. The classical ergodic axiom that assumes that the future is known and can be calculated as the statistical shadow of the past was one of the most important classical assertions that Keynes rejected. Instead he argued that when crucial economic decisions had to be made, decision makers could not merely assume that the future can be reduced to quantifiable risks calculated from already existing market data. Although in his discussion of uncertainty Keynes did not know or use the dichotomy between an ergodic and nonergodic stochastic system, in his criticism of Tinbergen's methodology he notes that economic time series cannot be stationary because "the economic environment is not homogeneous over a period of time." Nonstationarity is a sufficient but not a necessary condition for a nonergodic stochastic process. Accordingly, Keynes was implicitly arguing that economic processes over time occur in a nonergodic economic environment.

Taming Uncertainty in Keynes's Liquidity Theory

For decisions that involved potential large spending outflows or possible large income inflows that span a significant length of time, people "know" that they do not know what the future will be. Nevertheless, society has attempted to create an arrangement that will provide people with some control over their uncertain economic destinies. In capitalist economies, the use of money and legally binding money contracts to organize production and sales of goods and services permits individuals to have some control over their cash flows and therefore some control of their monetary economic future. Contracts provide the decision maker with some monetary control over major aspects of their cost of living today and for months and perhaps years ahead. Sales contracts provide business firms with the legal promise of current and future cash inflows sufficient to meet their costs of production and generate a profit. Individuals and business firms willingly enter into these contracts because each party thinks it is in their best interest to fulfill the terms of the contractual agreement. If, because of some unforeseen event, either party to a contract finds itself unable or unwilling to meet its contractual commitments, then the government judiciary will enforce the contract and require the defaulting party to either meet its contractual obligations or pay a sum of money sufficient to reimburse the other party for all monetary damages and losses incurred. Thus, for Keynes, his biographer Robert Skidelsky notes, "injustice is a matter of uncertainty, justice a matter of contractual predictability." In other words, by entering into contractual arrangements people assure themselves of a measure of predictability in terms of their contractual cashflows, even in a world of economic uncertainty. Arrow and Hahn wrote that "the terms in which contracts are made matter. In particular, if money is the goods in terms of which contracts are made, then the prices of goods in terms of money are of special significance. This is not the case if we consider an economy without a past or future.... If a serious monetary theory comes to be written, the fact that contracts are made in terms of money will be of considerable importance."[7]

Only Keynes's liquidity theory explaining the operation of a capitalist economy provides this serious monetary theory as a way of coping with an uncertain future. Money is that commodity that government decides will settle all legal contractual obligations. This definition of money is much wider than the definition of legal tender which is "This note is legal tender for all debts, private and public." An individual is said to be liquid if he/she can meet all contractual obligations as they come due. For business firms and households the maintenance of one's liquid status is of prime importance if bankruptcy is to be avoided. In our world, bankruptcy is the economic equivalent of a walk to the gallows.

Since the future is uncertain, we never know when we might be suddenly faced with a payment obligation at a future date that we did not, and could not, anticipate, and which we could not meet out of the cash inflows expected at that future date. Or else we might suddenly find an expected cash inflow disappearing for an unexpected reason. Accordingly we have a precautionary liquidity motive for maintaining a positive bank balance as well as for further enhancing our liquidity position to cushion the blow of any unanticipated events that may occur in the uncertain future. If individuals suddenly believe that the future is more uncertain than it was yesterday, then it will be only human to try to reduce cash outflow payments for goods and services today in order to increase their liquidity position to handle any uncertain adverse future events.

The most obvious way of reducing cash outflow is to spend less income on produced goods and services—that is to save more out of current income. This need for check-book balancing and desire for an additional liquidity cushion are irrelevant concepts for people who inhabit the artificial world of classical economic theory where the future is risky but reliably predictable. The efficient market concept ensures that no one in this mythical world would ever enter into a contractual payment obligation they could not meet since every person would know their future net income and spending pattern today and at every date in the future. If some participants do enter into wrong contracts, they are permitted to recontract without any income penalty—a solution that is not permitted in our world of experience. Efficient markets would never permit people to spend an amount that so exceeds their income that the debt cannot be serviced. Markets would not be efficient, if people today enter into contractual transactions that they cannot fulfill when the future occurs. Wouldn't credit-card holders who are having trouble meeting even their monthly minimum credit-card payment obligations and those sub prime mortgage borrowers who are being foreclosed out of their homes be happy to know they would never have become entrapped in such burdensome contractual arrangements if only they had lived in the classical world of efficient markets? In Keynes's analysis, on the other hand, the civil law of contracts and the importance of maintaining liquidity play crucial roles in understanding the operations of a capitalist economy—both from a domestic national standpoint and in the context of a globalize economy where each nation may employ a different currency and even different civil laws of contracts.

The sanctity of money contracts is the essence of the entrepreneurial system we call capitalism. Since money is that object that can always discharge a contractual obligation under the civil law of contracts, money is the most liquid of all assets. Nevertheless other liquid assets do exist; they have a lower degree of liquidity than money since they cannot be "tended": that is, handed to the party, to discharge a contractual obligation. As long as these other assets can be readily resold for money (liquidated) in a well-organized and orderly financial market, however, they will possess a degree of liquidity. A rapid sale of the liquid asset for money will permit people to use the money received from this sale to meet their contractual obligations. By orderly manner we mean that the price of the asset during its next sale will not differ by very much from the price of the previous transaction. As Peter L. Bernstein has noted, the existence of orderly financial markets for liquid assets encourages each holder (investor) of these securities to believe that he can execute a fast exit strategy at any moment when he suddenly decides he is dissatisfied with the way things are. Without liquidity for these stocks, the risks of being a minority stock holder (owner) in a business enterprise would be intolerable. Nevertheless the liquidity of orderly equity markets and its promotion of fast exit strategies make the separation of ownership and control (management) of business enterprises an important economic problem that economists and politicians have puzzled over since the 1930s.

In fact, Greenspan's surprise that the managers of large investment banks were not protecting the interests of the owners of these corporations indicates he does not understand the difference liquid markets make in driving a wedge between ownership and control. In classical theory there can never be a separation in the decision making between owners and managers.

In my paper "Securitization, liquidity and market failure"[8] I explain why, as long as the future is uncertain and not just probabilistically risky, the prices at which liquid assets can sell in a free market for at any future date can vary dramatically and almost instantaneously. A worst-case scenario is that in which liquid financial assets become unshakeable (illiquid) at any price as the market collapses (fails) in a disorderly manner. This is what happened in the mortgage-backed-securities (MBS) markets. To assure holders of liquid securities that the market price for their holdings will always change in an orderly manner, there must exist a person or firm in the market called a "market maker." The existence of this market maker assures the public that if, at any time, most holders of the financial asset suddenly want to execute a fast exit strategy and sell, while few or no people want to buy this liquid asset, the market maker will enter the market and purchase a sufficient volume of the asset being offered for sale to assure that the new market price of the asset will change continuously in an "orderly" manner from the price of the last transaction. In essence the market maker assures the holders of a liquid asset that they can always execute a fast exit strategy at a price not much different than the last price. In the New York Stock Exchange these market makers are called "specialists." Orderliness is a necessary condition to convince holders of the traded asset that they can readily liquidate their position at a market price close to the last publicly announced price. In other words, orderliness is necessary to maintain liquidity in these markets.

Modern efficient financial market theory suggests that these quaint institutional arrangements for market maker specialists are antiquated in this computer age. With the computer and the Internet, it is implied that the meeting of huge numbers of buyers and sellers can be done rapidly and efficiently in virtual space. Consequently there is no need for humans to act as specialists who keep the books and also make the market when necessary to assure the public the market is well-organized and orderly. The computer can keep the book on buy and sell orders, matching them in an orderly manner, more rapidly and at a much cheaper cost than the humans who had done these things in the past.

In the many financial markets that failed in the winter of 2007–2008 (e.g., the markets for mortgage-backed assets, auction-rate securities, and credit default swaps), the underlying financial instruments that were to provide the future cash flow for investors typically were long-term debt instruments. A necessary condition for these markets to be efficient is that the probabilistic risk of the debtors failing to meet all future cash flow contractual debt obligations can be 'known" with actuarial certainty. With this actuarial knowledge, it can be profitable for insurance companies to provide holders of these financial assets with insurance guaranteeing solvency and the payment of interest liabilities by the debtors.

In the classical efficient market theory, any observed market price variation around the actuarial value (price) determined by fundamentals is presumed to be statistical "white noise." As any statistician will tell you, if the size of the sample increases, then the variance (i.e., the quantitative measure of the white noise) decreases. Since computers can bring together many more buyers and sellers globally than the antiquated pre-computer market arrangements, the size of the sample of trading participants in the computer age will rise dramatically.

If, therefore, you believe in efficient market theory, then permitting computers to organize the market will decrease significantly the variance and therefore increase the probability of a more well-organized and orderly market than that which existed in the pre–computer era. In a world of efficient financial markets, holders of market traded assets can readily liquidate their position at a price close to the previously announced market price whenever any holder wishes to reduce his/her position in that asset. If the efficient market theory is applicable to our world, then how can we explain the failure of so many securitized financial markets wherein "investors are finding themselves locked into investments they can't cash out of?"[9]

Keynes's liquidity theory can provide the explanation. Keynes presumes that the economic future is uncertain. If future outcomes cannot be reliably predicted on the basis of existing past and present data, then there is no actuarial basis for insurance companies to provide holders of these assets protection against unfavorable outcomes. Accordingly, it should not be surprising that insurance companies such as AIG that have written policies to protect asset holders against possible unfavorable outcomes resulting from assets traded in these failing securitized markets find that they have experienced billions of dollars more in losses than they had actually estimated.[10] In a nonergodic world, it is actuarially impossible to estimate insurance payouts in the future. The existence of a market maker provides, all other things being equal, a higher degree of liquidity for the traded assets. But this assurance could dry up in severe sell conditions unless the monetary authority is willing to take direct action to provide resources to the market maker or, even indirectly to the market. If the market maker runs down his/her own resources and is not backed by the monetary authority indirectly, the asset becomes temporarily illiquid. Nevertheless, the asset holder "knows" that the market maker is providing his/her best effort to bolster the buyers' side and thereby restore liquidity to the market.

In markets without a market maker, on the other hand, there can be no assurance that the apparent liquidity of an asset cannot disappear almost instantaneously. Moreover, in the absence of a market maker, there is nothing to inspire confidence that someone is working to try to restore liquidity to the market. Those who suggest that one only needs a computer-based organization of a market are assuming the computer will always search and find enough participants to buy the security whenever there are a large number of holders who want to sell. After all, the "white noise" of buyers and sellers at prices other than the equilibrium price in efficient markets is assumed to be normally distributed. Hence, by assumption, there can never be a shortage of participants on one side or the other of financial markets. With the failure of thousands of security markets in the first weeks of 2008, it should be obvious that computers failed to find sufficient buyers. Moreover the computer is not programmed to enter automatically into failing markets and begin purchasing when almost everyone wants to sell at, or near, the last market price. The investment bankers who organized and sponsored the many mortgage-backed security markets will not act as market makers. These bankers may engage in "price talk"* before the market opens to suggest to their clients what the probable range of today's clearing price is likely to be. These "price talk" financial institutions, however, do not put their money where their mouth is. They are not required to make the market if the market clearing price is significantly below their "price talk" estimate. Nevertheless there are many reports showing that representatives of these investment banks have told clients that the holding of these assets "were 'cash equivalents' " (Kim and Anand[11]).

Due to this, many holders of these securities believed their holdings were very liquid since big financial institutions such as Goldman Sachs, Lehman Brothers, and Merrill Lynch were the dealers who organized the markets and normally provided "price talk." In an article in the February 15, 2008, issue of the *New York Times* it was reported: "Some well-heeled investors got a big jolt from Goldman Sachs this week; Goldman, the most celebrated bank on Wall Street, refused to let them withdraw money from investments that they considered as safe as cash....Goldman, Lehman Brothers, Merrill Lynch, etc. have been telling investors the market for these securities is frozen—and so is their cash."[12] Nevertheless, the absence of a credible market maker has shown the assets held by the participants in the market (believed to be liquid) can easily become illiquid! Had these investors learned

---

*Before the day's auction begins, the investment banker will typically provide "price talk" to their clients indicating a range of likely clearing rates for that auction. This range is based on a number of factors including the issuer's credit rating, the last clearance rate for this and similar issues, general macroeconomic conditions, etc.—Ed.

the harsh realities of Keynes's liquidity theory they might never participated in markets whose liquidity could be merely a mirage. Should not U.S. security laws and regulations provide sufficient information, so investors can make an informed decision in the future?

Notes

1. Davidson, P. (2008a): "How to Solve the U.S. Housing Problem and Avoid Recession: A Revived HOLC and RTC," *Policy Note*, Schwartz Center for Economic Policy Analysis January 2008; online at: www.newschool.edu/cepa or http://eco.bus.utk.edu/davidson.html

2. Davidson, P. (2008b): "Securitization, Liquidity and Market Failure" *Challenge*, May/June, 51 Volume 51, issue 3, pp. 43–56.

3. Samuelson, P. (1969): "Classical and Neoclassical Theory", pp. 170–190, in *Monetary Theory* edited by R.W. Clower, Penguin, London.

4. Lucas, R. (1981): *Studies in Business-Cycle Theory*, The MIT Press, Cambridge, MA: p. 27.

5. Ibid.: p. 276.

6. Keynes, J.M (1936): *The General Theory of Employment, Interest, and Money*, Harcourt, New York: p.16.

7. Arrow, K. and F. Hahn (1971): *General Competitive Analysis*, Holden–Day, San Francisco: pp. 256–257 (emphasis added).

8. Davidson (2008b).

9. Kim, J. and S. Anand (2008): "Some Investors Forced to hold 'Auction' Bonds," *Wall Street Journal*, February 21, p. D1.

10. Morgenson, G. (2008): "Arcane Market Is Next to Face Big Credit Test," *New York Times,* February 17, p. A1.

11. Kim, J. and S. Anand (2008): "Some Investors Forced to Hold 'Auction' Bonds: Market Freeze Leaves Them Unable to Cash Out Securities That Were Pitched as 'Safe'," *Wall Street Journal,* February 21, p. D1.

12. Anderson, J. and B. Vikas (2008): "New Trouble in Auction-Rate Securities," *New York Times,* February 15, p. D4.

CHAPTER 2

LESSONS FROM STATISTICAL FINANCE

Marc Potters

I want to shed some light on the current financial crises from the point of view of financial risk. By understanding the known failures of the classical model of Black and Scholes we can hope to unveil the pitfalls of more recent models such as copula models for CDO (Collateralized Debt Obligation) pricing. From this analysis we will realize that a major effect missing from modern mathematical models is the phenomenon of price impact and the resulting feedback loops between trading strategies and asset prices. I should state that my point of view is entrenched in my background as a physicist and a financial practitioner.

Modern Mathematical Finance

The birth of modern mathematical finance is the Black and Scholes paper of 1973. In the Black and Scholes model of the world, prices are continuous. There are no gaps or jumps; prices may fluctuate strongly but one can precisely define a continuous time limit such that the price at a certain instant is very close to the price at the next instant. The essence of this model is that fluctuations are Gaussian, and that large variations are extremely rare. For example, the 1987 crash had a negligible probability of occurring, even over the life span of the universe. The parameter that sets the strength of the fluctuations is called the volatility. It is constant in time, and known to market participants. The Black–Scholes model allows one to price options and, perhaps more importantly, to trade in such a way as to reduce the risk of writing these options. A remarkable result of the theory is that one should be able to follow a strategy (called the delta-hedge) such that the hedged portfolio is *riskless*. This is something Black and Scholes really wanted to achieve: to have a riskless instrument, since in that case the price of the option is unique. Another way to state this is: following the delta-hedge strategy on the underlying asset or holding an option is the exact same thing. This is called replication, which is perfect in the Black–Scholes world. This concept was at the heart of "Portfolio Insurance," to which we will return below. Black and Scholes however make a very important assumption that is not often fleshed out: when there is trading in their model (induced by delta hedging), it does not affect the price of the underlying asset.

Empirical Data

Fat Tails

The distribution of price changes of almost every asset is clearly not Gaussian, in particular at high frequencies. Empirical return distributions are more peaked at zero and have broader shoulders (fat tails) than a Gaussian distribution with the same variance (see figure 2.1). In practical terms, real markets regularly jump up or down by amounts so large that they would be deemed totally improbable by a Gaussian model such as the Black and Scholes one.

Note that the Gaussian distribution is clearly rejected by the bulk of the data. From the inset, one can see that even the Student and truncated Lévy distributions underestimate the extreme negative tails.[1]

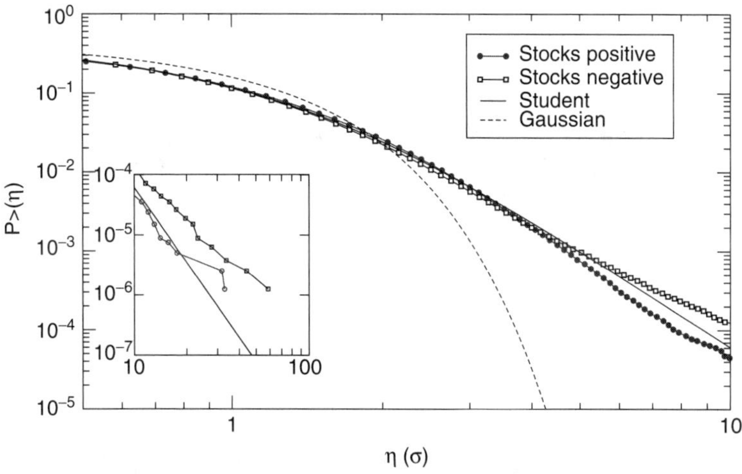

Figure 2.1 Cumulative distribution of daily price changes scaled by volatility for a pool of U.S. stocks compared to three distributions with the same variance. Positive returns and negative returns are plotted as two separate curves.

Volatility Fluctuations

As mentioned above, the Black–Scholes model assumes that the amplitude of the price fluctuations, what we call the volatility, is constant in time and known. But as illustrated in figure 2.2, the typical daily amplitude of price changes itself varies in time, with periods of high volatility and periods of low volatility. A popular model to describe these "fluctuations of fluctuations" is the Generalized Autoregressive Conditional Heteroskedasticity (GARCH) model, which assumes that volatility feeds back on itself and mean reverts to its average value in a given timescale. This means that volatility tends to persist over a well-defined, unique time scale. Empirically, however, there are many timescales—volatility can spike for a few hours or remain high for weeks, months, or even decades, as had happened after the 1929 crash. The top chart of figure 2.2 indeed reveals a big "blob" of volatility in the 1930s, it also shows the volatility spike of 1987 and if you look closely you can see the current

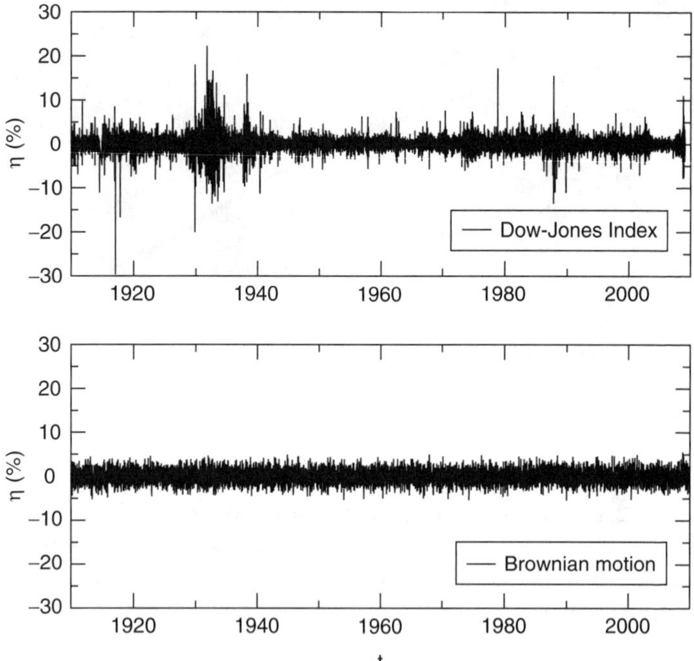

Figure 2.2 Daily returns of the Dow Jones Index since 1910 (top) compared to a simulated Brownian motion with the same variance (bottom). Note the large events and the clusters of high volatility present in the real data.

turmoil at the extreme right of the graph. Mathematically, the volatility correlation is well represented by a self-similar power-law in time, and exhibits what has been coined "long-range memory." This again is in stark contrast with a Brownian motion, which is the simulated process on the bottom chart of figure 2.2.

Option Hedging: A Case Study

I want to return to Black–Scholes and the most striking result of their model: if you delta-hedge an option, you get, in theory, zero risk, and perfect replication. We have simulated hedging an option on real data, in this case data on the Bund contracts although

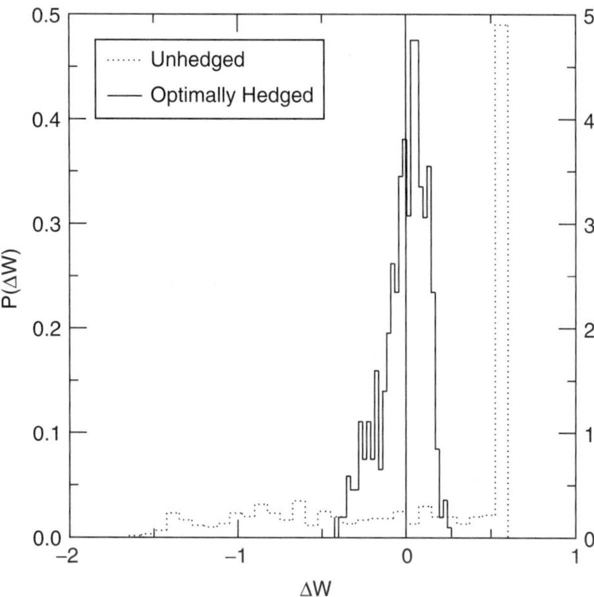

Figure 2.3 Distribution of profit-and-loss from writing a hedged (solid line) or unhedged (dashed line) option simulated with half-hour hedging on real data (Bund futures).

results are similar on many different types of assets. The Bund is not a particularly violent instrument; it is a future on German government bonds. If you sell an "at-the-money option" and wait for its expiry date without hedging it, about half the time, you get the premium, which in our study was about 0.6 point. The rest of the time, you pay something to the holder of the option, which can be as much as 1.5 or 2 points: see figure 2.3. You get an extremely asymmetric distribution, with a fairly large standard deviation of 1.05 points.

If you hedge the option using an optimal hedging strategy, which in the simulation was done every half an hour, you reduce the variance by a factor of three or four, but not much more. We are very far from zero risk in practice and the situation is much worse for out-of-the-money options.

The main failure of the Black–Scholes model, as I explained above, is its inability to account for risks that exist in reality, such as volatility risk. When you sell an option, you do not know what will be the realized variance from now until the maturity of the option. On top of that the price jumps, which makes the hedging quite ineffective. A crucial assumption that allows one to perfectly hedge an option is that the price process is continuous. This zero risk property does not hold in general, in particular if one uses realistic models of real data. Option trading involves some irreducible risk.

Market Impact

I am also a practitioner: our funds trade on supposedly liquid markets. We buy and sell rather large quantities of many different instruments. Because we buy large quantities of stocks, options, or futures, we can record the price before and after our trades and establish empirically that when we buy, we move the market up because of the impact of our trades (and vice-versa for sells). We want to come up with an accurate model of impact. Impact models, unfortunately, are rarely published, because the firms that have the data consider it to be proprietary. Nevertheless, there are some numbers and orders of magnitudes in the literature. We also have our own internal model and numbers. In a simple linear model of impact, buying a certain fraction of the normal daily volume moves the price by an amount proportional to this fraction. For example, buying or selling 10 percent of the normal traded volume of a stock moves the price up or down by roughly 0.5 percent. The linear model is not perfect but is a useful first approximation. More accurate models of impact are *sub-linear* in volume, meaning that as you increase the trading quantity the marginal impact decreases. This is true up to a point. There is also some evidence that for very large trades (trades that take more than 20 percent or 40 percent of the normal daily volume) the impact shoots up rapidly with volume and becomes *super-linear*. For the purpose of this paper all we need to know is that trading does impact prices, that this impact is quantifiable and that it is far from negligible for even moderately large trades.

Price Feedback Loop

The standard lore underlying classical models of mathematical finance is that prices are "god-given," or at least exogenous to markets in the sense that prices reflect accurately the fundamental "fair" value of assets. Hence, trading should merely reveal the price but not affect it. We have the opposite view: we strongly believe that prices are entirely determined by trading through impact—prices go up because people buy, and go down because people sell. For many assets, it is almost impossible to have an objective price within, say, at least a factor of two—this was Black's definition of an efficient market. The uncertainty (in the sense of Keynes) is such that the price of a company is not precisely knowable; only a rough order of magnitude estimate can ever be justified. The current price is therefore only the price just before you paid. But this price is used as a reference for the next transaction with a slight modification up or down depending on who is more aggressive between buyers and sellers. That process is self-sustained. The most important information people use for trading is the price. When they trade they impact the price, therefore modifying the decisions of other agents and eventually their own. That leads to feedback loops, which is the flip side of the impact phenomenon.

Negative and Positive Feedback

You can have negative feedback, which is a stabilizing phenomenon. If you have objective fair value—say, if you are a corporate raider and want to buy a certain company because you think you can extract some value out of it—you will only buy if the price is low enough. Alternatively, if you have a contrarian trading strategy, you will buy when the price goes down and sell when the price goes up. If you buy a significant enough volume when prices are falling you create demand for the asset, thereby inducing a price increase, or at least preventing a further fall. Conversely, by selling when prices are increasing you reduce demand which, in turn, puts a downward pressure on the price. Thus, a contrarian strategy keeps prices "in check". Most people who trade, though, have systems that tend to generate positive feedback. A large class of hedge funds use trend-following strategies. This is positive feedback which also occurs when the general public is affected by the collective mood. There are periods of euphoria—bubbles—when people start to put all their savings in the stock market because they are lured into thinking the stock market always goes up. Conversely, markets get bearish because investors sell their stock portfolio as a result of the market going down, leading to panic. Positive feedback loops clearly have a destabilizing effect. They lead to extreme valuations (e.g., oil at $150 per barrel in July 2008, or the price of the tulip bulb during the peak of the tulip mania, etc.), and finally to violent corrections and increased volatility.

Option Replication

Option replication is an important example of positive feedback. As we explained above, in a Black and Scholes model the pay-off of an option is exactly replicable by the delta-hedge strategy. So if you need the insurance provided by an option, you don't need to buy one, you can just "replicate" it by hedging. But the needed delta hedging is actually a positive feedback strategy: you sell when the price goes down, and buy when the price goes up. This was the scenario leading to the 1987 crash. People were selling these "replicated" options under the name "portfolio insurance." It was a popular strategy at the time, more than $80 bn of stocks were "insured" that way—compared to a total daily liquidity of around $5 bn back then. There was a small drop in the Dow Jones prior to the crash, which can be explained by some external economic news, but my point is that the crash itself, in view of the above orders of magnitude, was most likely due to the positive feedback.

The automated strategy was selling as the price was going down, pushing the price down further, an effect that was definitely not in the model. One of the shortfalls of the Black–Scholes model is that it does not take into account the possibility of large events, since their probability is so small. It is very ironic that the followers of the Black–Scholes model themselves created the largest event in the modern history of markets.

Long-Term Capital Management Collapse and Liquidity Risk
There is another type of feedback, which is the sudden correlation of otherwise uncorrelated strategies. In 1998, LTCM was a highly-leveraged hedge fund trading in different markets and doing different kinds of arbitrage that were uncorrelated in normal conditions. Initial losses in some strategies reduced their asset base and more importantly increased the perceived risk by their brokers, who then increased their margin requirement. This forced LTCM into deleveraging their positions. They started to push down the prices of all the assets that were they holding. So, even though all these assets were initially uncorrelated, they now became correlated; they all lost their value simultaneously, because of the actions of this one very large player, as well as very many copycats. It created a negative spiral, losses triggered deleveraging, and deleveraging generated more losses.

This brings me to liquidity risk. The lesson of LTCM is the importance of liquidity risk. You can have illiquid assets that are uncorrelated in normal times, but because they are illiquid, similar players may build large positions in them, all vying to pocket a liquidity premium. If they start to have substantial losses on some illiquid assets, they will need to deleverage and sell, generating further losses. Even if a certain illiquid asset was not affected by the initial loss, it may be contained in a larger portfolio that is deleveraged and therefore this asset could be subject to downward price pressure. In this scenario, almost all illiquid assets go down in a correlated fashion. These assets might be real–estate property in

Florida, structured debt of telecommunication companies, Russian bonds, or any asset that pays a premium just because it is illiquid.

Copula CDO Models and Moral Hazards

One of the lessons from Black–Scholes is one should first look at data before postulating a model on the basis of sheer mathematical convenience—in their case, a model that allows one to get rid of risk altogether and come up with a neat equation for the price of options with no ambiguity coming from residual (unhedgeable) risk. The very same thing can be said about the recent "copula" models for pricing credit derivatives. Here we are talking about the probability of simultaneous defaults: you buy a triple-A tranche of a CDO, which will only lose money if many underlying assets default at the same period. You need a model of simultaneous default, for which there is hardly any data, since even single defaults are by definition rather rare. People know how to deal with Gaussians, so they arbitrarily transform single "time to default" distribution into a Gaussian distribution. In this Gaussian world correlations can be introduced, which lead, when transformed back to the original problem, to a certain correlation structure for the time to default of the different instruments. But this has a completely obscure meaning, and intuition is lost. One can of course extract "implied" correlation parameters from market prices (even though these credit markets are not that liquid). But extrapolation to other instruments may lead to absurd results, exactly as the use of implied at-the-money volatilities would lead to absurd prices for out-of-the-money puts. Markets and traders have had thirty years to build some intuition about what was wrong with the Black–Scholes model and learn to deal with a volatility smile where the out-of-the-money volatility factors in the risk of large moves. But credit markets simply did not have time to build intuition about what was deeply wrong with these copula models before it was too late.

On top of the fact that people did not understand the models they were using, it turned out that they could make huge amounts of money by *not* understanding them. I think the demise of credit derivatives was much more of a problem of moral hazard than a problem of wrong models, or at least it showed that wrong models amplify moral hazard. Upton Sinclair said, "It is difficult to get a man to understand something when his salary depends upon his not understanding it." Traders and bank executives have effectively a call option on their profits and losses. It is often in their interest to take excessive risks, because the personal downside risk is limited.

Some Conclusions

Organization of Markets

Liquid, electronic, and anonymous markets, such as stock markets, futures markets, and options markets work quite well even if from time to time they go wild. But the probability of these large events can be estimated, so it is more "risk" than "uncertainty." Nobody defaulted on these markets in the recent period; the Chicago Mercantile Exchange (the CME) did not explode even when the S&P 500 dropped dramatically, and the Chicago Board Options Exchange Volatility Index (VIX) reached record highs. The system can handle risks, if large events and volatility fluctuations are included in risk models. The most dire failures occurred in the OTC (Over the Counter) market* which is basically much less liquid and transparent, being organized by brokers.

Feedback and Tail Correlations

One factor that is missing in most mathematical finance models is impact and the resulting feedback loops. This is especially the case in credit markets, where banks have bad assets on their books, many of which are actually credit derivatives related to the health of other banks. This is a huge feedback loop, which leads to enhanced tail

---

*In these markets trades of financial instruments take place directly between parties instead of through a medium such as the stock exchange.—Ed.

event correlations, for which there are no reliable models. It is true that there is very little data to build such models. One could argue that it is impossible to build such models, and that the simultaneous default of a large fraction of real-estate products in the United States did not happen to be a risk event, but an uncertainty event. I disagree, though; by thinking hard about mechanisms that can lead to correlations (interdependencies, liquidity, impact, etc.), it should still be possible to come up with better models.

Note

1. Adapted from: Bouchaud J.-Ph. and M. Potters (2003) *Theory of Financial Risk and Derivative Pricing*, Cambridge University Press, Cambridge.

AMBIGUITY AND ECONOMIC ACTIVITY: IMPLICATIONS FOR THE CURRENT CRISIS IN CREDIT MARKETS

Sujoy Mukerji

This chapter discusses some recent developments in economics regarding theories of decision making in conditions of uncertainty and argues that these new theories and models are singularly useful in explaining and understanding the ongoing credit crises. Moreover, it argues that the understanding based on these theories has significant policy implications about how the crises may be alleviated. While the formal articulation of these theories took place only recently, the ideas that formed their core had been discussed by Keynes[1] and Knight[2] in the 1920s. They had pointed out that for many important economic decisions, the decision maker (DM) faces "genuine" uncertainty such that he does not have reliable information about the relevant odds and that in such circumstances the uncertainty perceived by the DM may not be summarized by a single probability distribution, as in standard practice. It was also posited that a DM's choice behavior would also be determined by his taking into account how much he knew about the relevant odds. In decision making under conditions of uncertainty it is often the case that the decision maker's knowledge about the likelihood of contingent events is consistent with more than one probability distribution. For instance, if we happen to ask someone about the likelihood of a given eventuality, the answer we typically hear is a vague, "between x percent and y percent," rather than a precise, "z percent." The phenomena of vagueness, imprecision of one's subjective judgments or beliefs and its significance for decision making has vexed many eminent scholars, across a variety of disciplines, since at least the 1920s.

Not just economists, such as J.M. Keynes, F. Knight, and G.L.S. Shackle, philosopher–mathematicians such as I.J. Good, B.O. Koopman, and H.E. Kyberg also questioned whether subjective beliefs could be meaningfully represented by probabilities, while statisticians and decision–scientists such as L. Hurwicz, J. Hodges, E. Lehmann, C. Smith, and A. Wald constructed theories of decision making based on the hypothesis that in many situations the relevant uncertainty was too diffuse to be defined by an exact probability. Then, in the 1950s, L. Savage,[3] following on earlier work by F. Ramsey[4] and B. de Finetti,[5] made a pathbreaking contribution: Savage showed that if a decision maker's preferences (over acts) obeyed a certain set of axioms then her behavior could be represented as if she were maximizing expected utility with respect to some (subjective) probability. Hence, unless one were able to show that there were clear circumstances wherein it would be reasonable to behave in violation of one (or more) axioms and that many decision makers would actually behave so, it did not matter whether people's beliefs were probabilistic or not; we may, just as well, pretend that they were!

In a classic contribution, Daniel Ellsberg[6] came up with a pair of thought experiments, now famously called "Ellsberg paradoxes," which met Savage's challenge in precisely that manner. The examples showed there were circumstances in which it would seem reasonable for decision makers to let their behavior be affected by their knowledge of how well they knew the relevant odds. Next, we turn to an exposition of one of Ellsberg's two examples.

Consider the following experiment. Suppose there are two urns. It is known to subjects that each urn contains a mixture of 100 red and black balls. In urn I, the mixture is known to be 50:50. However, the subjects do not know the proportions of the two colors in urn II. A ball is drawn at random from each urn, generating events IR (i.e., a red ball is drawn from urn I), IB, IIR, IIB. DM is offered bets on these events. For example, £10 if IR, 0 otherwise. It is usually found that modal preferences in any particular experiment are: IR $\succ$ IIR* and IB $\succ$ IIB. It may be seen that such preferences are not expected utility preferences. Suppose, we assume $\Pr(IR) = \Pr(IB) = 0.5$. Then the preferences imply, $\Pr(IIR) < 0.5$ and $\Pr(IIB) < 0.5$. Clearly, a single probabilistic prior cannot express the aspects of uncertainty taken into account by the DM. In particular, a single prior cannot express the DM's concern that he knows relatively less about what the "true" prior is in urn II, a concern that affects his choice. The ambiguity-averse DM takes into account his subjective uncertainty about the odds and to what extent his choice is robust to this uncertainty. As Ellsberg reported, even when faced with the evidence that this was inconsistent with the Savage axioms most subjects stood their ground, "because it seems to them the sensible way to behave." Presumably they chose, to use the words of another famous economist P. Samuelson, "to satisfy their preferences and let the axioms satisfy themselves."[7] More generally ambiguity (or Knightian uncertainty) aversion is a commonly observed behavior that is inconsistent with expected utility. Essentially, decision makers are ambiguity–averse if they take into account how well they know the relevant odds and choose actions whose prospects are robust to the imprecision of their knowledge about the odds. Ambiguity, or lack of good knowledge of

---

*That is, drawing a red ball from the first urn is strictly preferred to drawing a red ball from the second urn).—Ed.

probabilities affecting contingent outcomes of a chosen action, is pervasive in economic decision making. It is not particular to the ill-informed and less sophisticated. Even a professional DM in a financial market knows it is often hard to distinguish (on the basis of historical data) between different models providing distinct (stochastic) forecasts of relevant financial variables. Such DMs may well think it is prudent to choose actions that take into account the uncertainty about the correct model. An example of such a robust decision rule is the Maximin Expected Utility theory, Gilboa and Schmeidler (1989)[8].

A basic version of the rule may be understood as follows. Suppose the DM identifies a set of probability distributions (on payoff relevant stochastic variables) consistent with available data. Let Π be the set of probability distributions deemed possible. Calculate the expected payoff of possible choice of action for each probability distribution π in the set Π. An action is evaluated by the minimum of possible expected payoffs. The rule asks that you choose the action with the maximum evaluation. Let us now turn to an example of a positive (economic) implication of this decision rule. The implication is that an economic agent who behaved in accordance with this decision rule will exhibit portfolio inertia. The result first appeared in Dow and Werlang (1993)[9]. Suppose a DM is offered a choice between a unit long and a unit short and a zero position on an asset which pays off contingent on the draw of a ball from urn II, as in the Ellsberg example discussed above. The following table (see Table 3.1) shows the contingent payoffs from each of the three choices.

Suppose the DM believes that the probability that a red ball is drawn (from urn II) lies in the interval [0.4, 0.6], with complementary

Table 3.1 Payoffs from Draws

Color of ball drawn from urn II	*Red*	*Black*
Payoff from a long position	10	0
Payoff from a short position	0	−10
Payoff from a zero position	0	0

beliefs about the event of a black ball being drawn. Applying the Gilboa–Schmeidler rule, it may be checked that the DM will evaluate the unit long position as $0.4 \times 10 = 4$; similarly, he evaluates the short position as $0.6 \times -10 = -6$. This implies that the DM will strictly prefer a zero position when market price lies in the interval $[-6, 4]$, thereby exhibiting a "portfolio inertia."

Mukerji and Tallon (2001)[10] develop this idea of Dow and Werlang in a general equilibrium model of a financial assets market with endogenous prices. They show that an increase in ambiguity or uncertainty, indicated by an increase in the size of interval of beliefs, increases incidence of no trade in risky assets by increasing the price interval where portfolio inertia occurs. Thus, the volume of trade/lending bears an inverse relationship to the ambient uncertainty. The uncertainty is triggered by unusual events and untested financial innovations that lead agents to question their worldview. More recently, Caballero and Krishnamurthy (2008)[11] present a model of crises and central bank policy that incorporates Knightian uncertainty. The model explains crisis regularities such as market-wide capital immobility, agents' disengagement from risk, and liquidity hoarding using an argument that, at its heart, relies on the logic of portfolio inertia explored by Dow and Werlang. The model hence provides an explanation for the current "seizure" of lending activity among banks based on Knightian uncertainty (aversion). This is an alternative explanation to an asymmetric information based "market for lemons" story. Arguably, the Knightian story is a better explanation: the increased uncertainty is about the valuation of securitized assets banks hold that are used as collateral for inter-bank lending. There is little to suggest that the *asymmetry* of information about such assets, between the bank holding the asset and the lending institution which takes it as a collateral, has increased even though the uncertainty *has*, in general, for both parties involved in the transaction of such assets. In this Knightian view of the crises, uncertainty ("counterparty risk") is the crucial variable that has caused the dramatic fall of lending especially between banks. The view is increasingly shared by leading economists and macro-economists, even those who do not necessarily work with Knightian models. This is exemplified by Olivier Blanchard's "Knight-time" in the *Economist*[12] and John Taylor's keynote lecture delivered in Ottawa on November 14, 2009, at a conference in honor of David Dodge, former Governor of the Bank of Canada. Taylor puts together, systematically, empirical evidence showing that the current financial crises is being driven by uncertainty, rather than liquidity problems. In what follows we reprise some of this evidence put forward by Taylor.

The financial crisis became acute on August 9 and 10, 2007, when the money market interest rates rose dramatically. A measure which has since become the focus of many studies is the spread between the three-month Libor and the three-month Overnight Index Swap (OIS). The OIS is a measure of what the markets expect the federal funds rate to be over the three-month period comparable to that during the three-month Libor. Subtracting OIS from Libor effectively controls for expectations effects that are a factor in all term loans, including three-month Libor. The difference between Libor and OIS is thus due to factors such as risk and liquidity effects, and not just interest-rates expectations. In the recent past, before the financial crises emerged, the OIS–Libor spread held at a steady level of about ten basis points. On August 9 and 10 of 2007 this spread jumped to unusually high levels and has remained high ever since. Of course, as Taylor argues, diagnosing the reason for the increased spreads is essential for determining what type of policy response is necessary. If it was a liquidity problem then providing more liquidity by making discount window borrowing easier or opening new windows or facilities would be appropriate. But if the issue was counterparty risk then a direct focus on the quality and transparency of the bank's balance sheets would be appropriate: either by requiring more transparency, dealing directly with the increasing number of mortgage defaults as housing prices fell, or by looking for ways to bring more capital into the banks and other financial institutions.

To assess the issue empirically, Taylor and Williams (2008)[13] looked for measures of risk in these markets to see whether they were correlated with the spread. One good measure of risk is the difference between interest rates on unsecured and secured inter-bank loans of the same maturity. Examples of secured loans are government-backed Repos between banks. By subtracting the interest rate on Repos from Libor, you could get a measure of risk. Using regression methods, Taylor and Williams then looked for the impact of this measure of risk on the Libor spread and showed that it could explain much of the variation in the spread. The results show a high correlation between the unsecured-secured spread and the Libor–OIS spread. There seems to be little role for liquidity. This suggests, therefore, that the market turmoil in the inter-bank market is not a liquidity problem of the kind that could be alleviated simply by central bank liquidity tools. Rather it is inherently a counterparty risk issue. This is not a situation like the Great Depression where just printing money or providing liquidity was the solution; rather it is due to fundamental problems relating to risk in the financial sector. This uncertainty-based understanding shows the need to combat the uncertainty problem by formulating policies for "qualitative easing" (see Wilhelm Buiter's blog). To take an example: this can be achieved by taking out toxic assets and swapping with sterilized debt, providing (government guaranteed) insurance for the toxic assets, deposit guarantees for inter-bank claims, and announcing longer term policies, etc. It is, to that extent, unfortunate that the focus of the economic policies in United Kingdom has been largely on "quantitative easing" and other such measures aimed at alleviating liquidity rather than on "qualitative easing" which tackles the problem of uncertainty-driven economic activity.

Notes

1. Keynes, J.M. (1921): *A Treatise on Probability*, Macmillan, London.

2. Knight, F. (1921): *Risk, Uncertainty and Profit*, Kelly, New York.

3. Savage, L.J. (1972): *The Foundations of Statistics*, Dover, New York.

4. Ramsey, F.P. (1926):"Truth and Probability," in Ramsey (1931), *The Foundations of Mathematics and other Logical Essays*, edited by R.B. Braithwaite, New York, Harcourt, Brace and Company; London, Kegan Paul, Trench, Trubner and Company, Ltd.,Ch. VII, pp. 156–198.

5. de Finetti, B. (1970): "Teoria Delle Probabilit`a," Volume primo, *Giulio Einaudi Editore*, Torino.

6. Ellsberg, D. (1963): "Risk, Ambiguity and the Savage Axioms," *Quarterly Journal of Economics*, 75: pp. 643–669.

7. Samuelson, P. (1950). "Probability and the attempts to measure utility," *The Economic Review*, July, pp. 169–170.

8. Gilboa, I. and D. Schmeidler (1989): "Maxmin Expected Utility with a Non-Unique Prior," *Journal of Mathematical Economics*, 18: pp. 141–153.

9. Dow, J. and S.R.C. Werlang (1992): "Uncertainty Aversion, Risk Aversion and the Optimal Choice of Portfolio," *Econometrica*, pp. 197–204.

10. Mukerji, S. and J.M. Tallon (2001): "Ambiguity Aversion and Incompleteness of Financial Markets," *Review of Economic Studies*, 68: pp. 883–904.

11. Caballero, R. J. and A. Krishnamurthy, (2008): "Collective Risk Management in a Flight to Quality Episode," *Journal of Finance*, 63(5), pp. 2195–2230.

12. O. Blanchard (2009): "Knight-time," *Economist*, January 29.

13. Taylor, J. B. and J. C. Williams (2009): "Black Swan in the Money Market," *American Economic Journal* Vol 1, issue 1, pp. 58–83.

PART II

MACRO-ECONOMICS AND THE CURRENT CRISIS

CHAPTER 4

MACRO-ECONOMIC FAILURES

Charles Goodhart

This chapter will focus on the implications of the current financial crisis for macroeconomic theory. With this aim, I shall concentrate on two main failures. First: the neo-Keynesian consensus three-equation Dynamic Stochastic General Equilibrium model (DSGE)—that we all love and I hate—that has been set out by macro-economists such as Gali and Gertler; and second: the Efficient-Markets Hypothesis (EMH).

1. DSGE Models

The so-called neo-Keynesian consensus was not Keynesian at all. It was essentially a real-business cycle model, with two added frictions. First was a pricing friction, which was discrete pricing.* Second was a monetary friction, "Get money into the system," which was cash in advance. There was not much in the way of good theory in terms of why one should have either friction though, clearly empirically, there are periods in which firms do not continuously reset prices, so empirically Calvo pricing, or

---

*Discrete pricing refers to a situation in which prices can only be changed at certain times.—Ed.

some such, is supported by the facts. Why in the world, in which this DSGE model prevailed, anyone should need cash, either in advance or otherwise, was never made clear; let alone money in the utility function, which was even more stupid. This model is supposedly based on micro-foundations, indeed this is its claim to fame; "You've got to base your macro-model on micro-foundations, rational agents optimizing, and so on." However, it required a nice little condition (that many people do not appreciate); that is the transversality condition, in order to simplify the model and to allow representative agents. But the transversality condition effectively says that by the end of the day, or when the model stops, all agents shall have repaid all their debts, including all the interest owed, with certainty. In other words, when a person dies he/she has zero assets left. What would be the point of keeping anything beyond death? This, however, also implies that all debts are paid. Nobody ever defaults.

Now, if nobody ever defaults, everybody has perfect zero credit risk, and everybody can borrow and lend at the single, risk-free interest-rate within the system. This effectively means you do not need any financial intermediaries, so you do not have any banks, you do not have any hedge funds, or anything like that. In fact, you do not need any money—at all. Because if everybody is perfectly risk-free, there is no credit risk whatsoever—everybody repays everything—all you need is some kind of information mechanism whereby the credits and debits are put into some kind of central computer and you work out at the end of the day how much in net you owe, or should get back. So when you step out of the taxi, the fact that you do not know who the taxi driver is, and that the taxi driver does not know who you are, does not make any difference, because you always repay everything—everyone repays all their debts. So all you do is put into this information mechanism an indication of how much is paid.

This obviously is not very realistic. There is no financial system, no banks; there is really no money, no default, and no credit risk.

This hardly looks like the world that we had in 2007–2008 when we had a lot of banks going bust, and we were rather worried about them. But the model works fine during good times; if you look at risk spreads during good times, these are more or less constant. Defaults on the whole are fairly rare, and people do not distrust their banks. So in fact, these DSGE models work really quite nicely when everything is going well. In addition we had a golden age between 1992 and 2007; it was the best age of economic development—for most advanced countries, at any rate—that we had ever seen. It is not surprising that in this particular period a model which entirely ignored default, credit risk, and banks etc., worked quite nicely. Such a model obviously does not work in all conditions, certainly not in the current scenario. In fact, the DSGE models are now a complete waste of time. So, in effect, from 2007–2008 all these models are of no significance or use whatsoever. Actually what is extraordinary to me is how much central banks were prepared to adopt and use models in which everything that a central bank ought to worry about in terms of default, bank intermediation, credit risk, money, etc., was simply *assumed* away! One of the problems that we have had in macro is that a bad but rigorous model tends to beat a correct but literary exposition in peer esteem in economics. What I would regard as a correct but literary exposition in economics is the work of Hyman Minsky.*

Minsky's theory was effectively sidelined by all the major macro-economists simply because there was no rigorous model attached to it. However, anyone involved with financial markets will realize

---

*Hyman Minsky was an American economist (1919–1996).Often described as a post-Keynesian, Minsky was particularly interested in understanding financial crises. He argued that financial market fragility needs to be understood in the relation to speculative investment bubbles inherent in financial markets. During times of economic expansion a speculative euphoria develops which leads to a rapid increase in debt. Once the debt exceeds borrowers' ability to pay back from their income a financial crisis erupts. The point in the business cycle at which investors face cash flow problems as a result of spiraling debt is often referred to as a "Minsky moment.".—Ed

that Minsky was right and that by default, the DSGE models were essentially wrong. Minsky, alas, is dead but at least we have a number of people trying to produce relatively rigorous models, incorporating default and credit risk as a central feature of their work and models. A much under-appreciated economist is Martin Shubik at Yale who has done, in my view, some of the best work on money, banking, and the interaction between monetary economics and macro, and his student Dmitri Tsomocos who is my colleague and one of Martin's best students, has also been doing much work on this, with which I have been helping, but it is Tsomocos's work rather than mine.

2. Efficient–Market Hypothesis

Let me next turn to the EMH, and not do this in theoretical but in practical terms. In the 1960s, for those of you who are old enough to remember it, banks' liquidity ratios were generally about 30 percent. Now in most cases they are about 5 percent and nearer 1 percent in the United Kingdom. How on earth did we allow banks' liquidity ratios to disintegrate, evaporate? Indeed, when I say 1 percent in United Kingdom, I think it was in 2007 when the U.K. commercial banks as a group held negative public sector debt. How do you hold negative public sector debt? You have borrowed more than you hold, and so it is perfectly possible. How did this happen? The main reason was that there was this massive trust in continuing access to well functioning, efficient, wholesale markets. So you could substitute funding liquidity through wholesale markets for market liquidity through asset holdings, and the general belief was that any bank or any financial intermediary could always access these wholesale markets as long as they were sufficiently well capitalized to assure solvency.

2(a) Basel II★

One of the problems has been that most people thought that Basel II would enable all the banks to be sufficiently well capitalized such that there would not be any doubts about their solvency. However, as we have learned, the banks, particularly the big international and big European banks—it was a European problem rather than an American problem—effectively manipulated and "gamed" Basel II in order to meet Basel II easily. Remember that Northern Rock was so well capitalized on a Basel II basis that the Financial Services Authority (FSA) regulators were prepared to allow it to increase its dividend at a time when its leverage ratio was over fifty times its equity base. Of course, everybody else, including bankers, knew that that it was wildly over-extended, whatever the Basel II ratio said, and began to worry about it. Even so, the point is that market prices can be driven by risk issues—liquidity risk, credit risk, and various self-amplifying spirals—well below fundamentals. What do I mean by fundamentals? I mean the present value of the expected future cash flows. Some of you will have recalled the Bank of England Financial Stability Review in April 2008 which effectively said that the price of almost all the mortgage-backed assets, Collateralized Debt Obligations (CDOs), and all the Residential Mortgage-Backed Security (RMBS) was actually currently wildly below any reasonable expectation of what cash flows might arise on the basis of a plausible, and even conservative expectation of future defaults.

2(b) Fundamentals

So how do prices move away from fundamentals? One way to think about this is as follows. You get an initial loss (in this case from the sub-prime mortgage market) and financial intermediaries, particularly those who are over-extended, run into funding problems because they cannot borrow in the wholesale markets, so they have to try to reduce their position, prices move away from fundamentals, they get greater losses, and the whole thing goes

---

*Basel II refers to the second of the Basel Accords providing guidelines for banking laws and regulations. It was initially published in June 2004.—Ed.

Table 4.1   Shows the increase in the percentage deduction from the net worth of a range of asset classes necessary to comply with SEC rules in connection with each long or short inventory position

Securities	April 2007	August 2008
U.S. treasuries	0.25	3
Investment-grade bonds	0–3	8–12
High-yield bonds	10–15	25–40
Equities	15	20
Senior leveraged loans	10–12	15–20
Mezzanine leveraged loans	18–25	35+
Prime MBS	2–4	10–20
ABS	3–5	50–60

Source: IMF Global Financial Stability Report, October 2008, p. 42

round again. You also have higher margin problems and, as you know, the margins have tended to increase by a factor of four or five in the current crisis (see Table 4.1) and equivalently those who are leveraged up on the basis of borrowing and collateral find they have to reduce their positions, and the whole thing gets worse.

The point of all this is that prices can move away from fundamentals. Effectively, if prices can move away from fundamentals, that means the end of the EMH for all practical purposes. The questions which then arise are: how can and why should prices move away from fundamentals? How can it happen that the market price actually moves away from the expected present value of the future cash flows?

2(c) Demonization of Assets

One of the answers, of course, is that everyone is very uncertain. Christopher Bliss's chapter talks about asymmetric information and that is certainly part of it. Another part of it is that markets can just virtually dry up and become dysfunctional. Another relevant case is when you get a market that is demonized, as much of the Mortgage-Backed Security Market (MBSM) has been demonized, people who could take these assets on board, like pension funds and life insurance companies, would find it very difficult to justify buying them to their trustees, even though the expectation of the future return on these if you can hold them to maturity is really quite positive.

Conclusion

So our major macro-models, our standard macro-models, our DSGE models that virtually everyone has been using, tell us absolutely nothing about our present problems and need to be reconsidered in total. Also, the EMH, on which a great deal of finance theory has been based, has come under well-justified and increasing attack. Considering that these are the two pillars on which macro-finance stands, there is a great deal that still needs to be done in the subject in order to try and get our models into some conjunction with the realities around us.

CHAPTER 5

HAYEK: ANOTHER PERSPECTIVE

Meghnad Desai

I want to talk about Friedrich Hayek because I believe he is the only person who has seriously rivaled Keynes in terms of business cycle theory, but who is completely forgotten now. Hayek's motivation was very straightforward. Having been trained in Vienna he was convinced that Walras was absolutely correct. But he also knew that there were business cycles. Therefore the question was: how do you reconcile Walrasian theory with observed business cycles? In fact he went, on his own money, to Columbia, to learn from Wesley Mitchell how to measure business cycles. He then came back to Vienna and became a Director of the Austrian Institute of Business Cycles.

Hayek said, "Obviously there is something in the world which is missing in Walras, and that is money." But he was convinced that he did not want to be just a "quantitative theory of money" sort of person; he did not want to believe, as in a standard Walrasian model, that money only explained the absolute level of prices. He wanted to trace the impact of money also on micro-economics in a general equilibrium framework, but also with heterogeneous capital. He really set himself a very ambitious program. The only other person to have done that was Marx, and he also failed, but that's another story!

The key lay in the Swedish economist Knut Wicksell's work; he had come across the same problem in reconciling the worlds of Ricardo and Walras. Wicksell's theory was that capitalism had this cumulative disequilibrium dynamics of business cycles; it was in the nature of capitalism to have cycles. His cycles were related to a gap between the natural rate of interest and the market rate of interest. (Hayek says that the natural rate of interest is actually the rate of profit, but Marx had given profit such a bad name that economists had to find other words for profit rate.) So the natural rate of interest is the profit rate in the economy. And the market rate is the rate at which people can borrow money. If they are equal, then money is neutral, and there is always equilibrium. But once there is a departure between the two, a disequilibrium sets in; if the market rate is below the natural rate there is a cumulative boom, and if the market rate is above it, there is a cumulative deflation.

Ludwig von Mises then took Wicksell's model and applied it to banking, asking how bankers gave loans to people. (There is no central bank in this lovely world.) He said that the problem is that bankers choose whether to give money to quick-yielding projects or slow-yielding ones. If the market rate is below the natural rate they are tempted to give money to long-yielding projects, because in Austrian theory the longer the production period, the more productive the technology. Hayek assumed that this was the essence of the problem. He modeled the entire economy as a single integrated firm in which labor was the only original factor of production; all capital was produced in the course of the production process (which began with labor alone in the earliest stage to the final consumption goods stage). In a steadily growing world, savings are always increasing, and this allows the technology (the period of production) to get "longer," that is, more productive. Thus, the integrated economy smoothly moves from shorter to longer production processes through the growth of voluntary savings. But credit creation enables more money to be invested in the longer projects than is profitable. The long economy drains resources, as it were, out of the short economy, but the long economy has not yielded output yet. So the short economy sees inflation because output of consumption goods falls, forcing up the prices of these goods. After a while this inflation accelerates and then something happens to make bankers panic. In those days they panicked because they had the gold standard and gold started leaking out of the system. When something like that happens the market rate abruptly goes from below to way above the natural rate. There is total breakdown in the economy because all the long projects are unfinished and are therefore abandoned. There is no longer money to complete them. The short economy cannot expand because the resources are not released by the long economy rapidly enough. So you have this long recession until the long economy releases resources. That was Hayek's model of the crisis. Along the way he talks about how, during the boom phase, banks make malinvestments, that is, they make investments that are not justified by the "fundamentals" because there are no voluntary savings. His description of what happens during the boom—about how people back projects that do not make sense and especially about what happens in a crisis, that is, the sudden rise in interest rates, and a credit freeze so that even good projects cannot find money—caught a lot of popular attention in 1931.

Keynes had written his *Treatise on Money* in two volumes and Hayek had written *Prices and Production*. Both started from a Wicksellian perspective. Some of the brightest economists at the time—Nicholas Kaldor, Evan Durbin, John Hicks, Hugh Gaitskell, and Douglas Jay—were Hayekians. Durbin, a young Socialist, suggested that if private banking was the problem the answer was to nationalize the banking system. This was not the answer that Hayek wanted! Hayek believed that cycles were caused by monetary disequilibria and the behavior of the people who gave out money or loans. Loan-giving behavior, especially loan-giving behavior in the face of a lack of voluntary saving, was the cause of crashes. (This is very much what has happened in the present crisis.) He didn't actually recommend a policy solution, because he did not believe in any. His answer was to wait it out. In his world, resources, excepting labor, were nonshiftable between the "long" and "short" economies. Labor had to be released, and all the losses of the "long" economy had to be borne, and then slowly resources would come back to the "short" economy and then once again expansion would take place. Thus you have a model of a transition from "short" to "long" economy, frustrated halfway through because of the monetary crisis.

Keynes does not have a banking system in the *General Theory*; only a consol that is the one asset the central bank sells and the public holds. So one would need to extend the Keynesian model to understand the present crisis. In the IS/LM framework I propose the following quick extension to the standard LM curve. The rate at which the government is willing give money is not the rate at which the banks want to give credit. To incorporate that you need another curve—a credit supply curve—which is slightly above the standard LM curve. And later on, in crisis, it gets much steeper. Although the government is cutting the interest rate, the credit supply moves to the left. So what you have, despite the government trying to cut interest and expand activity, is activity shrinking because of the credit supply function of the commercial banks. That will reconcile the standard Keynesian model with a banking crisis.

I have the feeling that the current crisis is very much a Hayekian crisis. The freezing up of the credit system—the need to recapitalize banks—is the Hayekian bit of it. The Keynesian part is the output recession. If there was only an output recession then we would know precisely what to do—Keynes has the answer to that—fiscal stimulus and so on. But what we don't have in the

Keynesian system is how to tackle the financial seizure in which credit is not available to commercial projects because of the output recession. This is where the current relevance of Hayek is. If Hayek was right—and I am not saying he is—then his idea was that reflation is counterproductive. That was the idea that made him unpopular, that reflation actually causes the problem to get worse, rather than better. This is because the long economy is sustained artificially to go on having to produce, while there is no economic logic for it. The relevance of this in the current crisis is that governments are seen to be very quickly shifting their story. About a year ago they subscribed to medium-run macro-economic responsibility, and were against high Debt/GDP ratios. And suddenly none of that matters anymore. The idea seems to be that you can suddenly tell a totally different story about how the macro-economy works, without actually giving an explanation for why the crisis has occurred. We have had recessions in the past, and Keynesian policy was very successful in the post-war period, with short recessions and short booms. Maybe 1971 was a sort of financial crisis, but the financial crisis we have now is a much bigger one than that. This is the first time that the crisis is not just national, but global, and that complicates matters. And this time the collapse of the inter-bank credit mechanism is much more serious than any in the last forty-five years.

This is a time when we need to examine whether it is possible that the current policy response is the wrong response; that this policy response, by putting a lot of money into fiscal spending and so on, will actually have a perverse reaction on the part of consumers. They have been lectured about Ricardian equivalence in one form or another for a long time; they have been told by the tabloid press for the last six months that "if you have a deficit, money will be clawed back from you." So it may be that, on the one hand governments are going to get into a worse fiscal position in terms of the budget balance, while on the other, consumers are going to be super-rational. I would say that they have longer memories than governments, and will say, "These guys are giving me money today, and tomorrow they will come and ask for it back, so I had better not spend it now or I won't have any money tomorrow." And so, just as banks are reluctant to lend to each other because of unknown counter-party risks, consumers are unwilling to spend because they do not know when they will be asked for the money back. The truth is that there are more models available than just the Walrasian and Keynesian ones. Economics was never uniform. Of course, even in the case of Keynes, there used to be multiple models out of Keynes, more than we have today. This is a very good time to dust off Hayek, because Hayek was trying to talk about a crisis in terms of the banking system being the principal source of trouble.

CHAPTER 6

GLOBALIZATION AND THE CURRENT CRISIS

Christopher Bliss

Prime Minister Gordon Brown is fond of saying that the current crisis for the British economy originated as an offshoot of the sub-prime debt problem that erupted in the United States. Although this claim seems a bit like the "Not me guv, nothing to do with me," line taken by accused villains, there is some truth in it. To understand how far it is true it is necessary to take into account the way in which the current recession differs from previous recessions, specially the two most recent ones in the early 1990s and the 1980s. What is not different is that like the recession of 2007–2008, both these recessions had a worldwide coverage. They were recessions of a globalized world economy. This was so even when, as with the bursting of the dot.com bubble, the United States was the leading driver of the downturn. The typical story of past recessions is that a booming economy displays increasing indications of inflation. Central banks raise interest rates, bubbles burst, and economies go into recession. This soon moderates inflation and recovery follows after two or three years. The 2007–2008 recession deviates from this typical story. At its start inflation was not high; it was at an unprecedented low level. There were bubbles, notably in stock markets and in housing markets, but this is now more obvious with the benefit of hindsight than it was at the time. This was inescapably a globalized world. China, if the name of a leading international player can serve as a short-hand for broader influences, was making its influence felt on rich countries. Cheap imports of manufactures were bearing down on inflation in these countries despite their high levels of capacity utilization. Responding to low inflation central banks cut interest rates and real interest rates were low. Add to this the downward pressure on wage rates in industrial countries that Chinese competition imposed (with help from the bias of technical change), and it is no surprise that corporate profitability was at the highest level seen for forty years.

Hubris and Regulation

The developments described above led many, who were by no means stupid, to think that a structural change had taken place that made the seemingly impossible perfectly sustainable. Apparently unending economic growth combined with low interest rates was seen to justify booms in housing markets (in Ireland, Spain, the United Kingdom, and to a lesser extent in the United States). The high corporate profitability projected forward made equities seem reasonably priced when they were actually expensive. Financial institutions were released from regulatory leashes, and the results seemed to be only positive. The private sector boomed, profits seemed to be enormous, and the tax revenues that followed were pleasing to governments. Capital markets seemed to work with great efficiency, and large-scale borrowing supported by loose collateral was commonplace. Hedge funds, private equity and gearing were high fashion. The new situation generated new institutions. Northern Rock was a new kind of building society, a bank, in that it relied mainly on the wholesale capital market for its loan funds. And it competed aggressively, offering better terms than its competitors, including cash-back deals that meant that loan to value ratios could be as high as 120 percent. All this was on Gordon

Brown's watch. His Financial Services Authority (FSA) was clearly not up to the task of assessing risk in the financial sector; indeed, it was dangerously complicit with Northern Rock. Also, an adverse judgment of regulators has to take account of the point that it is nearly impossible to criticize institutions when they are booming, seemingly untroubled, and hugely profitable. While rich countries were borrowing they were not saving to an equivalent extent. And some large countries (notably the United Kingdom and the United States) were running large current-account deficits. These deficits were financed by capital inflows from China, India, South-East Asia, and energy-rich countries. So the easiness of capital markets was the result of globalization.

A leading reason for the current credit crisis in the United Kingdom is that the easy credit line to overseas capital has largely disappeared. One of the great discoveries of economic theory during the last thirty years is that markets function poorly, if they function at all, in situations characterized by asymmetric information. For instance, when I buy a used car the seller probably knows much more about its quality than I can possibly know. I suspect that he is selling it because he knows that it is unreliable, although he may be selling it because he needs the money and can manage without a car. So the price that I, or anyone else, will be willingly to pay will be less than the "true" value of the car. This is where the U.S. sub-prime loan market is of central importance. U.S. banks, like those in other countries, were changing in character. The classic bank takes deposits and lends out funds to businesses and individuals. If well run, the assets (in the form of deposits) in its balance sheet exceed its liabilities. That difference makes up the bank's net worth: perhaps the capital put up by its original share-holders plus accumulated nondistributed profits. A bank is sound if its net worth is substantial. The problem of banking is that a sound bank borrows short and lends long. For that reason it remains vulnerable to a "run" on its deposits. If depositors decide in large numbers that they want to withdraw their deposits the bank cannot find the required liquidity quickly enough. This is where central banks in their role as lenders of last resort play a vital role. They discount the illiquid assets of retail banks; which is to say that they make the illiquid liquid. In theory this last service is extended only to banks with sound balance sheets on a long-term view. The above description is different from that which applies to a type of bank that may be called an investment bank. An investment bank uses capital provided by its share-holders plus funds borrowed from general capital markets to invest in a wide range of assets. These include company finance, especially new share issues, private equity buy-outs, mortgages, and much else besides. The soundness of an investment bank depends upon its net worth evaluated over a fairly long horizon. Short-term liquidity is less of an issue because funds are not borrowed to a great extent on a repayable-on-demand basis. The change in the character of banks mentioned above took the form of a blurring of the difference between retail banks and investment banks. Deposit-taking banks were permitted by alterations in regulations to issue mortgages and engage in businesses that were previously not allowed. One consequence of these developments was that bankers dealt more and more with investments about which they were less intimately informed and had less experience with. This development was encouraged by models of finance taught in business schools that said that risk should be moderated by the wide diversification of assets. This works if the risks of different assets are uncorrelated and if the investor can judge individual risks accurately. The problem in judging risks was supposed to have been alleviated by the rating agencies. If one of these agencies put a triple-A stamp on an asset it was taken to be an investment with a low risk of default. Another problem is that low correlations between the values of different assets evaporate in a big global crisis. As the late Ralph Vickers, of Vickers da Costa, once put it to me crudely but succinctly, "When the whorehouse catches fire everyone runs out." With the rating agencies it is true to say that the big worldwide problems did originate in the United States.

In short, the rating agencies became seriously corrupt. Originally they used to charge people who used their services for the ratings that they provided. In a globally interconnected world this became impractical. Party B could not be charged for information already provided to Party A, as once any party had the information it pretty much became general knowledge. Faced with this problem the rating agencies went over to charging the asset-issuers for the rating. But the agencies were by then profit-seeking firms that competed with one another. This inevitably led to a degradation of standards. Asset-issuers shopped around looking for triple-A ratings, and agencies that applied the highest standard and were the harshest in their risk assessments, made no money because originators would go somewhere else where they could get higher ratings. On top of these problems comes the development that assets have become more complicated. In the past Wal–Mart would sell corporate bonds and these would be rated triple-A on the basis that Wal–Mart was highly profitable and deemed unlikely to default. Now assets are often bundled together for convenience and reducing overall risk. This happened notoriously with U.S. mortgage debt, some of which was sub-prime, meaning that money had been lent to people who were unlikely to be able to repay it. Then all over the world such assets ended up on the balance sheets of banks that could easily borrow funds cheaply and thought that they were purchasing reliable sources of income. The sub-prime debts arrived bundled with various other assets, the whole package rated as sound. This was asymmetric information again. The banks were buying used cars that they could not judge themselves, relying on the salesman's sweet talk to authenticate their quality.

One often hears that the response to the current problems will be far tighter regulation in the future. To some extent that will undoubtedly be the case. It must be noted all the same that present problems owe much to past regulatory failure. And this is not surprising because regulators are victims of both their fallible human natures and also of that dreadful asymmetric information again.

A pernicious tendency is so-called regulatory capture (wherein interest groups and other political participants use the regulatory and coercive powers of the government to shape laws and regulations beneficial to them). To work effectively the regulator has to get close to his subjects as they surely know more about their (and hence his) business than anyone else does. However when you get close to people, you often come to respect them and to think as they do.

Global Imbalances

During the heady days of the great turn-of-the-century economic boom those who expressed serious doubts about the health of the world economy were in a minority. There was one issue, however, that made a majority of commentators wary. This was the huge U.S. current-account deficit and its twin brother the large-scale capital inflow into the United States. Other countries, notably the United Kingdom, exhibited a similar pattern, but the situation was at its extreme in the United States, and in any case the size of the U.S. economy gave this imbalance crucial significance. Current-account deficits and capital inflows are sometimes discussed separately as if they are unconnected. In fact they are simultaneously determined in a manner that can get quite complicated. The easiest way to see this is to consider a perturbation of an initial position, and to note how both current account and capital flow are affected in such a way that the balance of payments identity is preserved. Imagine therefore that U.S. households decide to spend a bit less and to save a bit more. An immediate effect is a small moderation in the rate of U.S. economic growth. There follows a small improvement in the U.S. current account, and possibly a small appreciation of the U.S. dollar against those currencies not tied to that dollar. An old Keynesian result is that the final rise in saving is less than the initial change in saving intention. This is because the moderation in economic growth itself lowers saving. Even so, there is now more saving than before, hence less borrowing. And if borrowing at the margin is all from abroad it follows that there will be an improvement in the capital account.

Prior to the current crisis two things were clear. First, the position could not continue indefinitely. Eventually, the United States, owing a mountain of dollar debt to the rest of the world, would surely create inflation to reduce its real burden. Foreseeing that, foreign lenders would in due course refuse to lend to the United States. Second, the imbalances could persist for some considerable time as long as China and other saving nations, needing somewhere to park their savings, could find nothing hugely more attractive than dollar assets—notably U.S. government bonds. The current macro-economic crisis has changed the picture substantially, and this will entail more rapid adjustment than was envisaged previously. Rich countries including the United Kingdom and now even Germany, led by the United States are planning large-scale deficit-financed schemes to reflate their sagging economies. Think what this means for the global balance between saving and borrowing. Rich countries particularly will be borrowing considerably more. From where will these funds come? China and the other big savers are experiencing recession just as much as the rich countries, so it is hard to see how they can plug the gap. The poor countries can borrow and they are going to be badly squeezed. This last point has received insufficient emphasis. But for the grand totals poor borrowing countries are marginal. The only other mechanism that can correct the balance of the world capital markets is a sharp increase in the cost of borrowing. That extra cost of borrowing can be thought of as, is indeed the same as, lower prices for corporate bonds. And lower prices for corporate bonds discourage private investment. So when governments borrow more, private investors borrow less. This is called *crowding out*. The term evokes the idea that if a large number of new visitors decide to go to a certain beach every Sunday, a significant number of existing users of that beach may decide not to go there. They will be crowded out. Notice that crowding out is not a one-for-one substitution. One hundred new visitors to the beach will not drive away one hundred existing users. It will typically displace less than one hundred, though it could conceivably displace more. The same is true of the effect of public borrowing on private investment. Crowding out in this context means that high public expenditure that moderates a recession comes with a price tag. That public expenditure has a discouraging effect on private investment, with the consequence that what is helpful now is unhelpful in the future. That is a not-uncommon pattern. Consider an idea that has been much promoted and already been implemented in Germany and in the United Kingdom. This is the payment of a subsidy to people who trade in old bangers to buy new cars. Plainly this helps motor manufactures and businesses associated with car sales. Yet while demand for the motoring industries is helped today, it is evidently suppressed in the future. Some old bangers that would have been replaced only in the next year in a normal case, are now being replaced this year because of the subsidy. If the global recession is short-lived the huge increase in borrowing need not matter a great deal. The borrowing will transfer wealth from countries that need funds to the few that are in a position to lend. If economic growth revives, this can all be unwound. Unfortunately current indications are that this downturn will be prolonged.

How Far Is Current Macro-Economics to Blame?

If macro-economics is to blame it is not for the crisis as such. It is for its failure to foresee the crisis and to recommend policies that should have been implemented well in advance to forestall our current problems. Many commentators on the current crisis have spoken of a revival of Keynesian economics, or of a return to Keynes. How can that be? Surely a majority of economists have been Keynesian since long ago. And cannot the same be said of central banks? This all depends on which Keynes one means, for there are at least two John

Maynard Keyneses in his *General Theory*, leave alone in references to his works by other authors. The Keynes most familiar to current students of economics is the inventor of the IS/LM model. Never mind that it was John Hicks who laid out that model and gave it its name. The model is drawn entirely from the pages of the *General Theory* and it represents the formal model of short period equilibrium with output determined by effective demand that was one of Keynes' great contributions. In forecasting inflation all central banks use some version of this model. Graduate students often study a version of the model that includes a central bank that uses a Taylor rule to set its interest rate. The IS/LM model has been criticized for not representing Keynes correctly. It would be better to say that it does not represent all of Keynes. In particular it is quite mechanical in its treatment of expectations. These can be fed into the model from outside, but doing so fails to capture the way in which the economic environment itself affects expectations. Keynes captures this idea in a passage that opens Chapter 16 of *The General Theory*:

> An act of individual saving means—so to speak—a decision not to have dinner to-day. But it does not necessitate a decision to have dinner or to buy a pair of boots a week hence or a year hence or to consume any specified thing at any specified date. Thus it depresses the business of preparing today's dinner without stimulating the business of making ready for some future act of consumption. It is not a substitution of future consumption-demand for present consumption-demand,—it is a net diminution of such demand. Moreover, the expectation of future consumption is so largely based on current experience of present consumption that a reduction in the latter is likely to depress the former, with the result that the act of saving will not merely depress the price of consumption-goods and leave the marginal efficiency of existing capital unaffected, but may actually tend to depress the latter also. In this event it may reduce present investment-demand as well as present consumption-demand.

A superficial reading of this passage would conclude that this is just the familiar multiplier at work, and that would be wrong. The multiplier is undoubtedly important, and we see it at work today as increasing unemployment cuts demand on the high street and elsewhere, and so leads to lay-offs and still more unemployment. Yet all that would happen even if we could freeze expectations and just let changes in demand do all the work. When a downturn is magnified by declining expectations it will be much worse, and probably more enduring. The most influential version of the IS/LM model in recent decades goes back to Edmund Phelps. There is one level of activity (employment) consistent with no change in the rate of inflation. This is the Non-Accelerating Inflation Rate of Unemployment (NAIRU). While based on a fine idea this model did not perform brilliantly, not even by the soft standard that applies to economic modeling. The problem is that there are several other influences that can impact on changes in the inflation rate. The effect of Chinese imports referred to above provides a good example. Where the approach did better is in the context of policies to slow down high or hyper inflation rates. No policy not involving a period of sharply reduced economic activity has ever been successful. This should remind us that every macro-model has its field of application, and may do badly outside its proper place. There is a warning there for people who think that all that is needed now is a new, more "Keynesian," less atomistic approach. Retro-fitting a macro-economic model to what has happened is not so difficult. The test is how well it will perform in the future.

Liquidity Preference

We see another Keynes at work when we examine his policy recommendations to counteract a depression. He was notably skeptical concerning the efficacy of monetary policy. The reason for this can readily be understood from his theory of investment. He rejected the orthodox (neoclassical) idea that investment decisions are guided by a simple calculus of net returns based on fixed and known cash flows. For Keynes investment decisions are more like the bets placed by punters at the race track. There are some objective factors, such as the known previous records of horses and jockeys. But these never suffice by themselves. In the end it is the love of risk and excitement that brings people to horse races and drives them to gamble. Keynes called this animal spirits (not because he was referring to actual animals, as with race horses), and his point was that this is a subjective influence, not easily affected by public policy. Keynes had another worry about monetary policy that has recently attracted increased interest. This is his famous liquidity trap. The idea is that purchases of bonds by the central bank might not raise their prices much if there is an overwhelming demand for liquidity. Then no private agents are buying bonds; they prefer to hang on to cash. While most private agents would like to sell bonds, there are no buyers. The market is one-sided and sellers are quantity-rationed. If the central bank buys, it eases the quantity constraint without much affecting the price. Then the encouragement of private investment that might follow from higher bond prices is not seen. The current crisis is not exactly the liquidity trap of the *General Theory*. It is very much a banking crisis. Bank failures were a notable feature of the 1930s, in the United States and elsewhere, but in principle one could have a liquidity problem without bank failures, given sufficiently low confidence. The banking crisis that is now a global problem (we can allow Gordon Brown that) arose because many major banks in major countries were effectively bankrupt. Yet no one was sure how far they were insolvent. To know that demanded a full audit and a valuation of their frequently dodgy assets. Governments piled in with open cheque books to save banking systems from collapse—which would be catastrophic. That worked but it did not restore banking systems to their old functionality. The global capital market is broken; being a "sound" borrower no longer ensures funding. That said, it is striking that the wounded British government is able to finance its ever-increasing borrowing at surprisingly good terms. This indicates a flight to safety. Government debt is seen as the best of a bad lot, because governments, unlike banks or corporations, cannot go bankrupt.

As noted above, the question of how much has to be injected into the U.K. banking system to make it function well involves taking into account the fact that the efficient international capital market, on which U.K. banks were heavily reliant, is no longer available. Is quantitative easing the answer? The Bank of England is already doing some of this, so we have to take the concept seriously. The idea is that the central bank buys (discounts) illiquid assets so as to feed liquidity into the banking system. Now that really does take us back to Keynes's liquidity trap. If would-be sellers of assets are quantity-rationed a limited amount of quantitative easing makes little difference. It is like a loosening of a ration. People can buy a bit more, but they are still rationed. A sufficiently massive quantitative easing exercise would suffuse the system with so much liquidity that the trap would be removed. But that is hardly feasible. It would involve, in the case of the United Kingdom, filling the Bank of England's balance sheet with a huge amount of junk. The Bank would become a version of Lehman Brothers, this time unable to file for bankruptcy.

Can We Solve the Global Crisis?

How bad might things get? They could become truly horrible if the world responds to current difficulties with protectionism. Then Keynesian policies might be too weak to stop a slide into mass unemployment. It is worth remembering that it was not Keynesian policies that lifted the world economy out of the depression of the 1930s. It was other things, in particular war, which is a scary thought. I think that there will be more protectionism, but my hope is that it will not become rampant, as in the 1930s. Those bad times are not forgotten. Even so, if this recession is deeply entrenched and prolonged it will be a hard test of the ability of governments to control declining economies. The reason for that can be found in the pages of Keynes's *General Theory*. Keynes argues that governments should bring about full employment, mainly by fiscal policy. In so doing they will make good the shortcomings of unregulated capitalism. What exactly is envisaged here? In the 1950s and 1960s macro-economists interpreted such policy as countercyclical activity; the government spending more when private demand is weak; less when it is strong. Unfortunately the evidence that accumulated showed that countercyclical policies performed badly. Their timing was unreliable, in particular because of unavoidable lags between change, observation, and policy response. When a failure to control inflation was added to the brew Keynesian economics seemed to be discredited. So if countercyclical policy is questionable we are left with macro-economic responses to big slow movements of the economy, such as would be seen with a deep, prolonged depression. Then there is a different problem: the government's long-run budget constraint. If the government counters the depression by spending more and taxing less, debt increases, and the interest on that debt itself becomes part of the deficit. Then either the deficit increases, or a given deficit has less and less effect, as more of it takes the form of debt service.

The classic answer to this problem is the balanced budget multiplier. A big government inflates the economy even if it runs no deficit, because all its expenditure translates into effective demand, and some of its tax revenue would have been saved. It is quite possible that a worldwide depression will be countered by bigger governments, accounting for an ever larger share of total demand. However, we already had big governments even before the current crisis began (especially in comparison with the 1930s). I doubt that we need worry too much about the problem of growing public sector debt. It is true that the current recession will be longer than earlier downturns. This is because on this occasion some big restructuring issues have to be addressed. These include fixing the banking system by sorting its underlying soundness, not just by throwing money at it; and also a rebalancing of household debt/income positions. The problem with the bank bail-outs so far is that they are extremely opaque. The billions put in by governments serve three purposes, and how much falls under each heading, and whether the total is sufficient, is not made at all clear.

First, some of the money is there to rescue banks from bankruptcy. This is distasteful but unavoidable. Some institutions really are too big to be allowed to fail. Governments, which is to say taxpayers, will not see most of that money come back. An insolvent bank may move into solvency, but this is an optimistic view. Even if banks are rescued from bankruptcy there is an additional need for funds, and this constitutes the second purpose of government aid. Learning from past mistakes it is now widely believed that banks in the past were under-capitalized; which is to say too reliant on outside credit markets. With private markets not functioning, only governments can recapitalize banking systems. If private markets recover some of this money may come back, but most of it surely will not. The third purpose of rescue funds is to make good the drying up of the intra-bank credit market, in particular its loss of free flows of funds from high-saving countries. With a return to more normal conditions some of these funds may be recovered. However, when the government stands over banks whipping them into increasing lending it runs the danger of debasing its own assets, in which case it will see less of its money come back. If intervention is clear and effective, recovery can follow. Modern capitalist economies are naturally dynamic. Technical change proceeds rapidly, and once growth revives excessive debt can be worked off over one or two decades. A mistake, to which the U.K. government has been prone, is to assume that we can somehow get back to where we were before the crisis arrived. That is not possible. The over-blown British financial sector cannot be restored to its previous level. The debt-financed consumer-spending-driven economy will not, and should not, come back. So what does our future economy look like? It is not easy to say; but in the case of the United Kingdom a leading force in the future will be import substitution. For an economy so wedded to imports the scope for import substitution is large, and the depreciation of the sterling assists it. And unlike exports, where the slowing of the world economy limits possibilities, the demand is already there, even in a depressed economy.

Another idea that deserves consideration is the economic historian's concept of long cycles. The present crisis may presage a sustained period of slower growth in the world economy. Until now growth always seemed to get faster. That boom and more booms however can now be seen to have been built on shaky foundations. Research concerned with the economics of happiness indicates that absolute income and its growth are not the most important variables. Insecurity and inequality are what matter most, as negative influences of course, in decreasing happiness. A less exciting but sounder world economy may not be a bad one to inhabit.

CHAPTER 7

GLOBAL IMBALANCES

Vijay Joshi

The current global economic crisis was triggered by the implosion of the wild credit boom that preceded it. The boom cannot be explained without understanding the micro-level dysfunctional incentives that permeated the financial sector. But that is not the whole story. The boom was also the product of macro-economic forces. The macro story goes back to the ex ante "savings glut" (or more accurately an excess of ex ante savings over investment) that in the last ten years took hold of economies of various countries such as Germany, Japan, China and East Asia more generally, and the oil-exporting countries, at various times, and for various reasons.

The East-Asian story is particularly relevant. There, the "glut" was related to two projects undertaken by these countries. The first project was to accumulate a large stock of foreign exchange reserves to insure themselves against a repeat of the capital flight they suffered in 1997–1998; the second was to keep exports growing rapidly in order to boost employment and growth. These projects were carried out by keeping exchange rates undervalued. East-Asian governments intervened actively and massively to buy dollars and resist market pressure for exchange-rate appreciation.

In addition, they sterilized their dollar purchases, thereby preventing the domestic price increases that would have otherwise eroded their export competitiveness by another route. The counterpart to export surpluses in the high-saving countries was the large American trade deficit, financed partly by private net capital inflows into the United States and partly but also significantly by the inflow of central bank reserves placed in U.S. treasuries. The United States was a willing partner in this enterprise. After the dotcom bust in 2001, U. S. interest-rates were cut from 6 percent to 1 percent and remained exceptionally low for three years; and there was, in addition, a fiscal boost. These expansionary policies, in combination with a distorted financial sector, produced a credit and housing bubble that was strong enough to withstand moderate interest-rate increases after 2004.

Though unintentional, there was a "virtuous" side to American expansionary policies: they stimulated demand, in the absence of which the savings glut in the rest of the world would have caused an American (and perhaps a world) recession. Of course, the ensuing huge rise in U.S. external deficits and debt was unsustainable. A dollar crisis would have been inevitable if the housing bubble had not imploded first.

That judgment about sustainability is controversial. Some economists were of the opinion that the global imbalance was benign, a manifestation of the superior productivity of the American economy and its magnetic attraction as a destination for the world's savings. But this smacks of a priori advocacy of the virtues of financial globalization. The facts speak clearly: America had a consumption boom, *not* an investment boom, in this century. Some other economists thought that the imbalance could have persisted for another decade or two since it suited the interests of both America and the high-saving countries. This seems implausible given the low return that central banks of the surplus countries were earning on their mounting dollar reserves. American economist and Director of the White House's National Economic Council Larry

Summers had it right when he described the situation as a fragile "balance of financial terror."

Whatever one's opinion about the durability of the counterfactual scenario, it can hardly be denied that, in the event, the global imbalance fed the American credit boom. Some of the capital inflows that covered America's current-account deficit went directly into sub-prime loans. Even central bank purchases of treasuries did so by an indirect route: central banks bought U.S. treasuries from American banks, which in turn used the proceeds to make sub-prime loans. And underlying these developments was the macro theme adumbrated above: both the global imbalance and the credit boom were the product of Keynesian full-employment policies in America, undertaken in part to counter the deflationary force that emanated from the "savings glut" in the rest of the world. We have to ask what macro-economic lessons can be drawn from the origin and build-up of the present crisis. Given the exogenous large rise in the propensity to save in parts of the world, was the crisis an inexorable Greek tragedy or could it have been avoided by better macro-policies?

The first lesson is that central banks must broaden their mandate beyond inflation targeting, narrowly construed, and pay attention to financial stability. In the United States., consumer-price inflation was low despite large excess demand, because of the massive trade deficit. But the pressure of demand was evident in asset-prices. It is clear that monetary policy must respond to credit and asset-price booms even if the consumer-price index is behaving itself. This cannot be done if the interest-rate is the only policy weapon. If central banks are to moderate asset-price booms, they need surely another one, for example, the ability to vary banks' capital charges in a counter-cyclical manner. There are also, in my judgment, good grounds for reviving the use of fiscal policy as a stabilization instrument, to be used fairly regularly, not just in emergencies. The second lesson is that we must abandon the fanciful idea that globalization has a built-in mechanism to avert excessive global imbalances.

But that thought leads to a hard question: Can policies be devised to prevent their emergence? Economic theory suggests an answer. The U.S. policy response to foreign excess savings was to engineer reflation. But this was crude closed-economy Keynesianism. Open-economy Keynesian theory tells us that the right response would have required action in both the United States and the surplus countries: tighter fiscal policy and exchange-rate depreciation in the United States, combined with looser fiscal policy and exchange-rate appreciation in the surplus countries. Easier said than done! But the closed-economy Keynesian alternative points toward a "Greek tragedy." Getting the appropriate pattern of global spending is difficult without international coordination of fiscal policies. If required on a regular basis, this would certainly be a tall order. But prevention of egregious excesses may require only occasional coordination. A necessary condition for such coordination is the engagement of systemically important emerging countries in global financial governance. They need to be given votes in the IMF that are commensurate with their economic importance. America and Europe will have to give up some formal control over the IMF in order to make it more legitimate and effective. Moreover, the IMF requires a new informal steering committee. The G7 will no longer do; it needs to be substituted by a more relevant grouping. Preventing excessive imbalances will also require a more satisfactory exchange-rate system than the one we have now. Current exchange-rate arrangements impede international adjustment. Ever since the IMF Articles were amended in 1978, each country has been allowed unilaterally to choose any exchange-rate regime that suits its goals and circumstances. (The amended Articles also forbade "exchange-rate manipulation" but that provision has never been clearly articulated, let alone enforced.) We have ended up with a free-for-all that is radically flawed from a systemic viewpoint. Undervaluation may make individual sense for a single small country but it is dangerous nonsense if practiced by a key country or by several significant countries. (The future relevance of this point is that in the next quarter century, as emerging countries catch up with the West, major exchange-rate changes will be necessary in response to fast productivity growth in their tradable sectors. Smooth realignments are unlikely if the present free-for-all continues.) It is crucially important, therefore, that after the present crisis has subsided, the major countries agree on a common exchange-rate system that promotes balance of payments adjustment. (Small countries tend to follow one major country or the other.)

What common system should they choose? A fixed exchange-rate between major currencies is one possible alternative, provided sterilization is prohibited. But it would involve a total loss of monetary autonomy. It would also imply adjusting to large, asymmetric disturbances—such as the differential rates of productivity growth already alluded to—by internal price changes. This would be politically unacceptable as well as economically painful and inefficient. So the major currencies will have to float. But unmanaged floating has a severe downside: it can sometimes lead to prolonged and manifestly insane exchange-rate movements (for example, the U.S. dollar bubble in 1984–1985) that can themselves cause macro-economic instability. That leaves only two realistic options. Exchange-rates between major currencies could float in an unmanaged fashion most of the time but with occasional macro-economic policy cooperation and coordinated exchange market intervention to prevent gross misalignments. Or, more ambitiously, the major countries could agree periodically on reference exchange-rates that are appropriate for global adjustment, intervention being permitted only if undertaken to influence market exchange-rates in the direction of reference rates. It is no good relying on the IMF, as presently constituted, to set up such a scheme. But it could be done by a reformed IMF, led by the key countries.

If we assume, realistically, that we will not have clean floating, the new exchange-rate system will have to be supplemented by some way of providing reserves to countries without their having to earn them by running trade surpluses (or to acquire them by borrowing expensively on the world capital market.) Is it not time to activate the IMF's power to create international fiat money (Special Drawing Rights)? This would be a straightforward way of meeting countries' reserve needs for crisis insurance. It would also reduce future dependence on the use of national currencies as international reserves and thereby tighten the balance of payments constraint on reserve-issuer countries. The generous line of credit enjoyed by the United States, currently the main supplier of global reserves, clearly contributed to the present crisis by tempting it into a spending spree.

PART III

MODELS, METAPHORS, AND MORALS

CHAPTER 8

KNOWLEDGE IN ECONOMICS

John Kay

What can we know about the economic world? What is the nature of knowledge in economics? As I see it, the test of an economic model is whether it is useful rather than whether it is true. Let me elucidate that theme in relation to the two basic models which underpin much of financial economics.

The Efficient-Market Hypothesis

The first model is the efficient-market hypothesis or the EMH. Whether the EMH is true or false is not a dichotomy that should be considered. The EMH is neither true nor false. Buffett and Keynes actually have more aphorisms about investment and finance than any other two people in the world. Warren Buffett made a particularly useful observation, "Observing correctly that the market was frequently efficient, they," he wrote, referring to the academics and investment professionals, "went on to conclude incorrectly that it was always efficient. The difference between these propositions is night and day." I think that gets to the heart of the matter—in the case of Buffett, to the heart of the $60 bn that he made in the interstices in which markets were not efficient. It is a mistake to believe the efficient-market theory is false. The insight that information is essentially incorporated in prices is important. It is an equally big mistake to believe that the EMH is true. Market prices do not necessarily represent a considered, weighted assessment of available information. Everyone who looks at financial markets ought to know about and use the EMH, but people have made big mistakes both from believing the EMH and from disbelieving it.

The second model that is neither true nor false is the prevailing approach to risk and uncertainty. Everyone who has been trained in economics has been trained to look at risks in terms of subjective probabilities, which are formed on Bayesian principles. These probabilities are combined with expected utilities of some sort to make up what taken as a whole is described as the theory of subjective expected utility. It is essential to know that theory if you are dealing with financial markets. It is a mistake to think it false, and may prove to be an expensive mistake. But it is also a mistake to believe the theory is true. Both the EMH and the theory of subjective expected utility are theories that are illuminating, useful, but not true. That is the nature of knowledge in economics. Good theories are theories that are useful—no more, no less.

Models and Metaphors

I have come to believe that the best theories in economics are theories like the Prisoner's Dilemma or Akerlof's lemons model. They are metaphors and models rather than realistic descriptions of the world. I once described the Akerlof lemons' model at a conference. Someone in the audience who was attending on behalf of the RMF (the trade association for used-car dealers in the United Kingdom) said that the description that I had given was a monstrous slur on the integrity of used-car dealers. It is well known that these traders are among the most honest and respectable people in the United Kingdom. But he had, of course, missed the point; not just in the sense that what he said about used-car dealers does not correspond to most people's experience, but also because the Akerlof model is not about used-car dealers. Even if used-car dealers were people of the utmost integrity, that empirical fact would not affect the power or relevance of the model in any way. Nor is it relevant that a sheriff who behaves as the character in the *Prisoner's Dilemma* does would probably breach the Human Rights Act. To debate whether these stories are true or not, something that the representative of the RMF was in effect doing, is absurd. These models are metaphors. The lemons model and the Prisoner's Dilemma are models that are useful in the sense that, once they have been understood, the ideas that underlie them can actually be applied to a wide variety of situations. The skill of the economist is to understand which models are relevant for particular situations. The mastery of this skill—or the lack of mastery—is of particular relevance to the crisis that we have, and to an academic understanding of its origins and consequences.

The main causes and issues in the crisis are to do with the results of securitization and resecuritization in wholesale money markets. There are broadly two competing descriptions of what has been happening in these markets over the past ten years. One account is based on a model of efficient risk allocation. The result of the endless packaging and repackaging of risks into yet more carefully-structured packages is that we have been able to devise ways of reducing the costs of bearing risk to historically low levels. The other account is that the attractions of these instruments arises mainly from asymmetric information. People who understand well what they are doing have sold packages to people who understood them less well, and therefore overvalued them. Debate between these two schools continues. I believe the latter explanation is far more illuminating, and that events have borne out this interpretation. But, depending on which theory you subscribe to, there is a big difference in the policy you adopt going forward. Now we do not actually have to choose between these two models. I think there is an element of truth in both. Securitization markets would never have come into being if there had not been some validity in the risk allocation model. But these markets grew to the scale that they achieved because of an asymmetry in information.

Economic *versus* Anthropological Models

I learned that one did not have to choose between models by reflecting on a discussion I had many years ago in Oxford with a group of anthropologists. We had come together to talk about what anthropology could contribute to economics and business. The meeting was not as productive as I had hoped. But after it we all went off to the pub. Someone ordered a round of drinks and we got into a scholarly discussion of why people ordered rounds of drinks in pubs. For the anthropologist the question was easy. This was ritual gift exchange of a kind they had observed in many remote and primitive tribes. For the economists too the question was easy. The practice of buying rounds was a way to minimize transactions costs. The number of occasions in which you had to visit the bar was reduced. I then came up with a test of these alternative hypotheses. I asked "Did you feel you had won or lost if you had bought more drinks during the evening than you had bought back for you?" I discovered that the anthropologists thought the idea was to buy more drinks than you received. The economists thought the objective was the other way around. I learned that it is a good idea to go out for drinks with anthropologists rather than economists. But not much more, until I reflected and realized that the two hypotheses are not competing or conflicting explanations. The sort of social institutions and conventions we have conform to the taxonomies that anthropologists observe across a variety of cultures. But if these practices were not functional rather than dysfunctional in an economic sense they probably would not persist. Both the economic and anthropological explanation were part of the story but neither constituted the complete story.

I am arguing that the way we should think of models and use models in economics is to accept many different models. We ought to have a toolkit. The skill of the economist is in deciding which of many incommensurable models he should apply in a particular context. Both the EMH and the theory of subjective expected utility are valuable in particular contexts, and inappropriate in others.

Probabilistic *versus* Narrative Approach

Let me elaborate that latter issue. There are two broad, competing ways of thinking about risk and uncertainty. I now know that I have sat through many discussions that have been blighted by fundamental mutual misunderstanding about the interpretation of risk and uncertainty. Such discussions are confrontations between people who have been trained as economists to think about risk and uncertainty in one way and people who have been brought up in the practical world of business and finance and tend to think about these questions quite differently. If you have been trained as an economist, as I have been, you have learned the approach I described earlier. You attach probabilities to the different possible outcomes of a risky process; you update these probabilities in a sort of Bayesian manner; and you apply these probabilities to calculate expected utilities.

But most people actually do not think about risk in this way. They think about risks in terms of narratives and stories and the validity of these narratives and stories. What an economist regards as risk will be dispersion around a mean. What a businessperson regards as risk will be the likelihood of the nonfulfillment of a particular narrative. That narrative is somewhere in the upper-part of the distribution of possible outcomes.

Two Standards of Proof

By being involved as an economist in legal cases I learned one way of seeing the difference between the probabilistic and the narrative way of thinking through. In English and American law there are two standards of proof. In both countries, the criminal standard of proof demands that guilt be established "beyond reasonable doubt." The standard required in civil cases is different. The English phrase is "on the balance of probabilities." The American phrase is "on the preponderance of the evidence." Interestingly, and significantly, lawyers generally seem to assume that "the balance of probabilities" and "the preponderance of the evidence" mean pretty much the same thing. For someone who has been trained in classical statistical theory or economics, it seems easy to explain the meaning of these standards. "On the balance of probabilities" means the relevant probability in excess of 0.5. Beyond reasonable doubt means 0.95 or 0.99 or some similarly large number. Yet it is perfectly clear when you talk to a lawyer that he or she interprets the issue differently. In order to make a case in a legal process, you have to tell a story. The issue of standard of proof is the issue of how much confidence the judge or the jury can have in any particular story. The "balance of probabilities" in their vocabulary means that the plaintiff's argument is better than any other plausible story that might be, or at least has been, told. Beyond reasonable doubt means the account is a very compelling story indeed. The standard of proof is a measure of confidence in a story. This was the way Keynes and Knight thought about uncertainty in the 1920s. And it is very different from the way economists like me have been brought up to think about risk.

Keynes and Knight or Ramsay and Savage

Keynes and Knight lost while Savage and Ramsay won the argument about the way to view risk The key point is that the Keynesian/Knightian school of thought which views issues in terms of confidence, narratives, and degrees of belief in narratives in an uncertain world has become wholly unfashionable. Modern economists, rather, ignore uncertainty by reducing it to risk founded on Bayesian beliefs about future events in the way that Ramsay and Savage posited. I believe that both these streams of thought are powerful ways of thinking about risk and uncertainty. Neither approach is true: both are illuminating.

The world is uncertain as well as risky. Let me spell out that distinction. Risk implies we can think about probability distributions because we can define a range of outcomes over which we can identify probabilities. Uncertainty means we are not able to describe intelligibly even the range of outcomes. In a world which is uncertain, not merely risky, the narrative approach is often a more useful way of taking things forward.

Behavioral Economics

That leads me to behavioral economics—which is an important way of taking economics forward. But the way in which it does so is often misinterpreted. In behavioral economics, we observe how people behave and what they do rather than imposing normative models of how we think people ought to behave. That approach answers a common and justified criticism of economists. It is a criticism encapsulated in the joke: if you asked an economist to study the behavior of horses, he would sit down at a desk with a blank sheet of paper and ask, "Now what would I do if I were a horse?" The model is imposed *a priori:* genuine empirical enquiry is ruled out.

Rationality

Behavioral economics has been largely predicated on the belief that people behave "irrationally." The problem that arises, I thought, was best expressed in the title of one of the successful pop books about behavioral economics—there have been several in the last year or two. If one adopts the title *Predictably Irrational*, one should start asking hard questions. In an evolutionary world we would not expect predictable or persistent irrationality. If behavior does not correspond to our models of rationality, perhaps the problem lies with our models of rationality rather than with the behavior which we are actually studying.

Cognitive Mistakes

Example One

Let me give some examples. A pop book on behavioral economics starts with a signature example: "Suppose you are in a helicopter above Los Angeles without a chart and you want to fly to Reno,

Nevada. What direction would you fly in?" Rather surprisingly Reno, Nevada, is to the west of Los Angeles not to the east. You should fly west rather than east. Make this a real problem rather than an abstract problem. First of all if you were in a helicopter above Los Angeles without a chart you should and would be grounded straight away by the Federal Aviation Administration. Further, if you were really to go by road from Los Angeles to Reno, Nevada, the best way to go is to follow Highway 5 north and then turn east on Highway 80 at Sacramento to reach Reno.

So if you were in the helicopter you should go the same way. If you were to fly directly from Los Angeles to Reno, Nevada you would bump into Mount Whitney, the highest mountain in the United States and would not make it to Reno. The way we organize our thinking is to think of U.S. highways as being organized on a north, south, east, west grid. If we do not have proper directions to follow, these practical mechanisms are more useful than the topographical knowledge that the author laughs at us for not having.

Example Two

Another classic experiment in cognitive mistakes posits a triangle that says "A bird in the the hand." Most people who are asked to read this quickly say, "A bird in the hand" rather than the correct description which is, "A bird in the the hand." But who is actually making the mistake in this particular experiment? It is far from clear that the subject rather than the experimenter is in error. All of us are used to the idea that people do not quite say exactly what they mean. We use our general knowledge to make sense of what we hear. "A bird in the the hand" does not make any sense; "A bird in the hand" does. Almost every day I pass, at Baker Street Tube Station, a Transport for London sign that says, "This way for the buses to Stansted Airport"—spelled "Stanstead." I have never asked, "Oh that's interesting. Where is Stanstead Airport? I wonder whether useful services go from there." I know perfectly well what is meant. We apply our general knowledge. We bring extraneous information to bear. That skill is immensely valuable in navigating complicated environments. It is a skill that we find very difficult to replicate with computers or other analytic devices. An analytic mistake does not necessarily equate to an operational mistake.

Example Three

My last example is this: a famous behavioral economics problem known as the Linda problem. It runs something like this. Linda is single and lives alone. She was actively involved in demonstrations against Shell, in the Brent Spar affair during her studies at Anglia Polytechnic University. Now which of the following do you think is more likely? (1) Linda is a bank manager, (2) Linda is a spokesperson for the Animal Liberation Front (ALF), (3) Linda is a bank manager and an active feminist. If you try that on an audience— and I have tried it on several—you typically get roughly equal numbers going for each of the three options. People who have been brought up the way most of us as economists have been brought up would then say, "Anyone who gives the second or third answers is stupid. It can't be more likely that Linda is both a bank manager and an active feminist than that she's a bank manager. Everyone knows that compound probabilities cannot be greater than simple probabilities. So the third answer has to be wrong. If you say she's more likely to be a spokesperson for the Animal Liberation Front, you are falling victim to what is known as the base-rate fallacy. You haven't taken account of the fact that there are only about two people who speak for the ALF, but there are tens of thousands of bank managers. The likelihood of someone being a bank manager is so much greater than that of a person being a spokesperson for the ALF that the second answer too cannot be right.

But I think most people interpret the question in a Keynesian/ Knightian sense. "Which is the story in which you have most confidence?" is what they would ask. In that frame of mind, you will very plausibly give either the second or third answers rather than the first. There is something incongruous about the first answer. But the second and third answers, in some senses, cohere.

Conclusion

There are two fundamentally different ways about thinking about uncertainty. The narrative approach to uncertainty is every bit as compelling as the Bayesian probabilistic way of thinking about risks. There are some situations in which one, or the other, is the more appropriate. The mistake we have made, as academic economists, has been to believe too much in particular models of the economy—to suppose our models are true rather than just illuminating. We apply useful models to situations to which they are inappropriate in the mistaken belief that these models are, in some sense, true. That is the link between the two issues that we deal with in this book—the state of economics and the current crisis which we are in. The route ahead is for us to be much more eclectic in the set of models we use.

CHAPTER 9

MODELS AND METAPHORS

Richard Bronk

This chapter discusses the role of metaphors and models in structuring our view of the world. I will touch on some of the same topics that John Kay, interestingly, mentioned earlier. Let me begin by saying why I first become interested in the subject.

For seventeen years I worked in the financial and business world. The longer I did so, the more I became aware of a mismatch between the way economists usually model economies and interpret data, and the way markets often seem to operate in practice. When I looked at the markets and economies, I saw dynamic and creative systems characterized by relentless product innovation, constantly surprising new options and self-reinforcing emotional spasms of euphoria and despair. Yet, for the most part, economists relied on equilibrium models to make predictions; they assumed that, despite the uncertainty engendered by frequent innovations and increasing returns to small events, individual actors can optimize the utility (within any given set of information and other constraints) on the basis of rational expectations. To me, it seemed increasingly evident that successful investors and entrepreneurs rely as much on having an intuitive grasp of emerging patterns and on imagining how the future might be as on any rational calculation; and they are often in the business of dreaming up new strategies and new techniques every bit as much as maximizing the efficiency of tried and tested ones.

In trying to make sense of all this, it seemed natural to me to turn to the thinkers who had done most to explore the nature of creativity, imagination, and sentiments, namely the Romantics. It increasingly struck me that it was possible to derive from the great Romantic poets and philosophers of around two centuries ago an alternative perspective on markets—a new set of grounding assumptions, models, and research methods that could help us understand better how creative markets work and how economic agents operate in conditions of uncertainty. The end result is *The Romantic Economist*, published in February 2009 by Cambridge University Press.

What I want to focus on here though is just one aspect of the ideas I develop in this context; namely, the lessons we can draw from Romanticism about the role of metaphors and models in structuring our view of the world.

The Romantics inherited from the German philosopher Immanuel Kant an understanding that the world-as-it-appears-to-us is, to some extent at least, a creation of our own minds. Any particular observation you make is the joint product of the sense data your mind receives and a conceptual structure that your mind constructs. As Wordsworth put it (in "Tintern Abbey" and "The Prelude"), your mind half-creates what it sees; it is a "creator and a receiver both." In his "Table Talk," Coleridge expressed especially beautifully the necessity of our minds providing a "principle of selection" if we are to make any sense of the chaos around us, when he said, "You must have a lantern in your hand to give light, otherwise all the materials in the world are useless, for you cannot find them and, if you could, you could not arrange them."

The trouble, though, with Coleridge's lantern, or with any theory or metaphor, is that the light it casts, the focus it brings, is limited and partial. This means that if you suffer from theoretical dogmatism and use only one set of models, one source of light, you will keep stumbling on aspects of reality that are outside the area illuminated by your theory or model. As Coleridge reminded us, "No simile runs on all four legs" and, likewise, the metaphorical coloring implied by using any particular model to study social reality always implies some distortion as well as focus.

Now, you might ask are models really just another form of metaphor? That depends, of course, on how they are used. As a pure mathematical construct, a model may make use of metaphors—equilibrium, for example—but models can also become metaphors in themselves if they are applied to make sense of social reality—not an uncommon use.

When you interpret real-world events in terms of a model, and collect and assess data to plug into that model in ways that conform to the categories allowed for in the model, you are structuring your vision and analysis in a certain way. If the model seems to be useful, you may soon forget how necessarily stylized this picture is. Before long, observations may become unconsciously theory-soaked, unconsciously colored by the model or metaphor you have internalized.

For this reason, I argue in *The Romantic Economist* that all social scientists, and especially economists, need to become both more aware of how the metaphors and models they use structure their analysis, and be more willing to experiment with different ways of seeing the world before they settle on one interpretation.

If you deconstruct virtually any work of standard economics or Rational Choice Theory, you will quickly find it littered with metaphors. The theories are themselves often giant metaphors—think of Game Theory, for example—or, they may employ a whole panoply of concepts derived from a nonsocial context, especially Newtonian or nineteenth-century physics—"equilibrium," the "elasticity" of prices, the "velocity" of money, utility "functions," production "factors," and so on. All these metaphors buried deep in the models of standard economics have made it resemble, as Philip Mirowski put it in *More Heat Than Light* (1989), a sort of "social physics."

The fact that so much economic theory is constructed on the mechanical metaphor of equilibrium, and on the supporting assumption borrowed from utilitarianism that individuals predictably optimize within given constraints, has profound effects on the way economists see and understand the economy. The essence of their perspective becomes a matter of the relative efficiency of allocation, the degree of market failure, and the nature of incentives. These are, of course, all important facets of economies, but they are not the only ones that deserve notice and analysis.

Now, if instead you experiment with metaphors from biology, as Alfred Marshall advocated, from modern Complexity Theory, or from Romantic organicism, your attention will immediately be directed to the dynamism of the economic process and its interdependence with society at large. Because these metaphors have a ready place for novelty—with new ideas behaving like DNA mutations—and they readily encompass increasing returns and tipping points—with creative destruction behaving like evolution or mass-extinction events—we will suddenly see these sorts of dynamic facets of the economy all over the place. At the same time, we will have the modeling tools at hand to analyze the social formation of preferences and behavior. Notice though, crucially, that these new organic metaphors cannot explain the allocative efficiency of many markets that was isolated so effectively by mechanical models and metaphors. Instead, their focus illuminates other aspects that are often important: the self-reinforcing interdependence of social and economic factors, and the frequently unpredictable and nonlinear impact of novelty, and human ingenuity. In other words, my message is that no one model or metaphor can reveal everything we need to know.

Before we explore further how to use these insights about the structuring role of metaphors to develop the theoretical structure of economics and give us new pointers for best research practice, it is worth highlighting the topicality of this issue for current economic policy. Social reality is not an independent variable against which we can assess the usefulness of different theories: it is partly constructed by the theories we employ to think about it. To put it another way, all social scientists are seeking to interpret a pre-interpreted world, in which the beliefs and behavior of individual agents are structured by the dominant theory-based structures of interpretation of their day. The metaphors and models that economists use have a habit (for good or ill) of influencing the beliefs and actions of policy makers and entrepreneurs alike. This means that if you want to explain market behavior and government policy responses you need to understand the theories and metaphors that the key actors have internalized.

When it comes to explaining the current economic crisis, there are two important examples of this influence of models on behavior.

First, it is at least arguable that one reason that few central bankers, Treasury officials, or financial market participants anticipated the crisis is that most of them had come to assume that the Greenspan approach and neo-classical models were all they needed to use. As a result, they were not predisposed to see the problems that were emerging, since their theoretical and conceptual frameworks had no place for them. The moral of the story is that there is never only one right way of looking at the world: we need always to be humble enough to admit that no single theory that we develop can illuminate all aspects of a problem. Nor can it provide in itself a full and sufficient template for action.

A second example relevant to this economic crisis is the use of a set of models by bankers that purported to turn uncertainty about the future into measurable risk. The emphasis placed on these models reflected an intellectual failure, in my view, to understand the extent to which novelty and frequent innovation actually create uncertainty by introducing new elements into the equations of life. There was, in retrospect something absurd in relying so completely on risk models based on correlations trawled from data on the past at the very moment when bankers were creating new complex products each and every week. For innovation disturbs systematic regularities of behavior and breaks many of the predictable links between the past and the future.

Again the moral of the story is that we should never rely on one set of models to chart our way through the unknown future. Although models may help us see some things more clearly, they do leave blind spots. Now let me return briefly to the ways in which experimentation with new metaphors can help us develop new models and new approaches in economics. A new metaphor can do more than shake us out of habitual ways of looking at a problem by suggesting a new conceptual grid for making sense of reality. In many cases it can also suggest new mathematical models that might help us analyze markets. For example, there is much that financial market modelers can learn from epidemiology in trying to model irrational exuberance and financial panic. The nonlinear equations, self-reinforcing dynamics, and sensitivity to tipping points are similar in the two contexts: disease epidemics and market behavior. Indeed, in some cases, importing a whole new metaphorical structure—for example, based on organicism rather than mechanics—may lead to an entirely new paradigm or perspective on markets.

Here there is a very important distinction to be made between improving (or amending) an existing conceptual framework and shifting to a new one. Very often what economic modelers do is to co-opt new metaphorical elements from a quite different discipline or modeling tradition, and apply them as a series of bolt-on amendments to their preferred existing theoretical framework. This is usually done in the name of remaining true to the central rationalist micro-foundations of neo-classical economics (with its assumption that individuals rationally optimize, within given constraints, on the best information and probability forecasts available). An example of this is Endogenous Growth Theory, which does attempt to build in Schumpeter's creative destruction, but without dropping the modeling assumption that individuals and firms are rational, probability-calculating optimizers of consumption and profit.

But how can these micro-level assumptions sit comfortably with seeking to understand a world made uncertain by the vagaries of human inventiveness and the increasing returns to innovation? It seems to me that the result of this sort of piecemeal co-option of metaphors from other contexts is to introduce a certain internal logical confusion at the heart of economic models. I would argue that it is much better to stick with mechanical metaphors and models (based on the assumptions that markets tend to equilibrium, and that individuals predictably optimize their position) where this seems to elucidate and forecast what is going on; and then switch to completely different organic metaphors and correspondingly different micro-foundations where they do not.

In a nutshell my thesis is that where economists are trying to model markets characterized by creativity, uncertainty, self-reinforcing emotional reactions, or behavior that is conditioned by social norms, they need to switch to using more organic dynamic-systems models, such as those used in Complexity Theory. And at the same time they need, correspondingly, to switch from *homo economicus*—Economic Man—to *homo sociologicus* and *homo romanticus* as micro-level models of motivation to explain behavior at the individual level. What I am suggesting here is that, rather than seeking to explain everything in the economic arena through one paradigm, one set of theoretical spectacles, we should instead learn how to be more disciplined in our use of different paradigms or theories, with the choice of theory driven by the nature of the problem we are studying.

We should refrain from endlessly amending our preferred paradigm until, as Thomas Kuhn put it in *The Structure of Scientific Revolutions* (1962), it resembles late-Ptolemaic astronomy—a monstrous "system of compounded circles" whose "complexity was increasing far more rapidly than its accuracy." Instead, we should be willing to use different paradigms, and different theoretical structures, to explain different problems, different aspects of our socio-economic predicament. In this way, we can get the benefit of the focus brought by each pure theory, without suffering the myopia caused by using the wrong spectacles in the wrong situation. Of course, if this more eclectic approach is to work, we have to be disciplined in establishing the boundaries of applicability for each type of model. We also need to be careful to ensure that our initial assessment of the nature of a research or policy problem is made from the perspective of several different paradigms or theories. And I set out some pointers to how this can be done effectively in *The Romantic Economist*.

Some people have commented that such a multi-paradigm approach is all very well, but wherever you depart from the normal micro-foundations of standard economics, the analysis stops being economics, and becomes sociology, or perhaps political economy. Here, it seems to me, the economics profession has a choice. Either it can remain true to its central mechanical metaphors of equilibrium and utilitarian assumptions of rationally optimizing individuals, in which case it will explain much about our economies very well, but about other aspects very poorly, as it does now. Or, it can return in a more disciplined form to an older version of political economy, such as that practiced by Adam Smith, which was broader in focus and technique than today's science.

Economics as a discipline, in other words, has to choose whether it wants to give up its imperialist ambitions to explain and model everything in the socio-economic sphere or, alternatively, to become more broadminded in its use of different types of model and metaphor.

Before I conclude, let me dwell briefly on the role of mathematics in economic analysis. It is, of course, the case that many of the greatest insights of economics have come from hunting down the logical consequences of assumptions with mathematics. But the use of mathematics is not entirely unproblematic. The mathematical language in which most economics is currently developed and expressed can itself structure the way economists see and analyze the world, so that nothing is seen as relevant unless it can be reduced to numerical or algebraic notation. It need not, however, be this way. If only economists would heed the advice of the father of modern economics, Alfred Marshall, and translate their findings and assumptions back into English—or French, or German, or Spanish for that matter—then they would avoid the pitfalls of relying solely on a language and conceptual structure different from that employed, for the most part, by economic agents themselves. What is more, if economists translated their work back into English, as much as possible, their assumptions and methods would be open to audit by those in other disciplines and professions.

This would help allow for better inter-disciplinary research among academics, and a higher likelihood of informed challenges by academics in other fields to the assumptions and methods used by economists in particular contexts.

The same "back-to-English" rule applied in the finance world would have probably helped prevent some of the crisis we now face. For example, if more senior bankers, regulators, and politicians had focused on the fact that many of the risk models behind the structured products used by banks' trading desks assumed as a matter of course that the past was a good predictor of risks in the future—even in fast, innovating markets—they might have become uneasy enough to blow the whistle just a little sooner.

CHAPTER 10

ECONOMICS AND MORALS

Edward Skidelsky

The first principle of economics, wrote F.Y. Edgeworth in 1881, is that "every agent is actuated only by self-interest." Edgeworth's principle has hung like a cross round the necks of economists ever since. Taken as literally descriptive, it implies an intolerably cynical view of humankind. Yet taken as a purely theoretical postulate, it is unclear how theorems derived from it could have any relevance to actual human affairs. One might as well, jibed the author John Ruskin, construct a science of gymnastics upon the supposition that men have no skeleton.

To such perplexities the modern economist has a ready retort. Edgeworth's principle may indeed have underwritten classical economics, bound up as it was with the psychological hedonism of Bentham and his disciples, but economics has long since shed such associations. In its modern form it rests simply on the assumption that humans choose between competing ends, that their choices reveal their preferences, and that those preferences can be consistently ordered.

About the *content* of those preferences, it is silent. They may be self-interested or altruistic, devilish or saintly; the laws of economics hold good all the same. "Imagine," asked Lionel Robbins, a pioneer of this approach, "a community of sybarites visited by a Savonarola. Their former ends become revolting to them. The pleasures of the senses are banished. Surely economic analysis is still applicable. There is no need to change the categories of explanation; all that has happened is that the demand schedules have changed. The 'pig philosophy'—to use Carlyle's contemptuous epithet—turns out to be all-embracing." As this last sentence suggests, Robbins's redefinition of economics helped both to liberate the discipline from dubious psychological assumptions and to greatly broaden its scope. These two developments went hand in hand. Classical economists had confined themselves to the sphere in which their hypotheses of rational egoism held *prima facie* truth, namely that of tradable commodities. They did not, with the notable exception of Malthus, broach the noneconomic side of life. But once economics was defined in terms of the formal properties of choice itself, the path was open to its universalization. Robbins himself remained an economist in the traditional mould, but the seed he had sown was to bear fruit in Rational Choice Theory and its many offshoots.

Today any human behavior, provided it is quantifiable and can be exhibited as a choice between competing ends, falls potentially within the scope of economics.

So can Edgeworth's first principle finally be laid to rest? Well, not quite. The abstract heights of rational choice theory may presuppose very little in the way of empirical psychology, but its concrete applications cannot avoid making specific assumptions about human nature, and those assumptions remain by and large egoistic. The works of Gary Becker, Richard Posner, and Mancur Olson provide many examples. And this raises a puzzle. If the assumption of egoism is not integral to economic theory, why its persistence? Is it a mere residue of nineteenth-century hedonism? Or should it perhaps be taken as a maxim of prudence, a modern version of Kant's principle that political institutions are best tailored to devils rather than saints? Neither answer is wholly adequate. The truth, I shall argue, is that egoism remains implicit in the *method* of economics, even if it no longer features explicitly as a first premise. Cast out of the front door, it has been smuggled in again through the back. Indeed, egoism in modern economics assumes a form far subtler and more pervasive than any envisaged by Edgeworth. No longer confined to the grossly material realm of commerce and industry, it now permeates the whole range of human purposes, right up to and including the most "spiritual." In this respect, economics faithfully mirrors a broader social development, dubbed "the triumph of the therapeutic" by the sociologist Phillip Rieff.

So in what sense does economics remain methodologically egoistic? A brief scenario may help illustrate the point. Imagine that Mary, a Catholic, goes to church every Sunday, while her husband, an atheist, stays at home. Then Mary acquires a lover. The only time they can meet without raising suspicion is Sunday morning. Here, then, is a classic economic dilemma in Robbins's sense. Mary has a scarce resource—time—and two competing ends. So after consulting her utility function she decides to see her lover three Sundays a month, and go to church on the remaining fourth; an optimal solution, given the constraints.

The scenario is of course absurd, and deliberately so. Mary's dilemma is not one that could be handled by economic theory, for going to church and seeing a lover are not assessable along a single dimension. If going to church is good, as opposed to merely pleasant, then seeing a lover is not good at all. Similarly, if seeing a lover is good, then going to church is sheer hypocrisy, whatever warm feelings it engenders. Going to church and going to see a lover are, in a word, incommensurable. To accept the one as good is to commit oneself to a moral system according to which the other is bad. No trade-off is possible. Mary's choice is a stark one; one might even say a tragic one, although that would be a bit melodramatic.

Yet there is one circumstance in which an economic analysis of Mary's predicament might become appropriate—namely one in which Mary brackets out the question of goodness altogether and considers only the relative intensity of her wants. She might, for instance, decide that her desire to see her lover, although stronger than her desire to go to church, is nonetheless outweighed by the guilt she will feel if she neglects the faith of her fathers, and so on. But whatever she chooses, it will be determined by the balance of her own inclinations, not by the goodness of the thing chosen. Only if Mary adopts this essentially therapeutic attitude to her own predicament will it appear as an economic problem, open to a calculative solution.

I hope it is now clear why I believe egoism is implicit in the method of economics, whether or not it features explicitly as a first principle.

Most human ends are incommensurable, in the sense that the acceptance of one as good implies the rejection of others as bad. Yet the economist must, in obedience to the logic of his discipline, treat all ends as commensurable. He must assess them along a single dimension. And the only dimension available for this purpose is that of the ego and its wants. The diversity of human goods is thus reduced to a series of benefits of varying degrees of magnitude. And this holds true even of the so-called higher goods, such as friendship, science, faith, and so forth.

Without explicitly denying their uniqueness the economist must—simply by putting them in the scales alongside other, more material, goods—surreptitiously convert them into "benefits," thereby emptying them of their distinctive significance. So Robbins is disingenuous in claiming that economics has outgrown its hedonistic origins. The pig-philosophy may have proved all-embracing, but a pig-philosophy it remains. Gary Becker, I think, provides a good illustration of the way the logic of economics tends to egoism, whatever the intentions of the individual economist. Like Robbins, Becker claims to make no assumptions about the content of preferences. His analysis assumes that individuals "maximize welfare as they conceive it, whether they be selfish, altruistic, loyal, spiteful, or masochistic." But because Becker also assumes that "ethics and culture affect behavior in the same general way as do other determinants of utility," that is, that all ends are commensurable in the sense defined above, his position ends up indistinguishable from that of Edgeworth. For instance, it is of no fundamental significance for Becker whether the costs attaching to a particular activity take the forms of fines, imprisonment, or feelings of guilt; all are negative utilities to be thrown into the scales together. But this is fundamentally to distort the character of moral reasoning. A truly moral person is not one who, having discovered a lost wallet, weighs the cost to his conscience against the benefit to his bank balance, and finds the former heavier. Rather he just discounts the benefit to his bank balance. Now whether such honest people actually exist is irrelevant; my point is conceptual, not empirical. A motivational structure of this sort is implied by the concept of honesty. Becker's analysis of morality in terms of costs and benefits leaves us with something unrecognizable as morality.

It is a consequence of what I have said that the economic approach cannot be valid as a general theory of human behavior. Most human ends are incommensurable; they come freighted with moral and cultural meanings. They cannot, without distortion, be reduced to the common coin of subjective satisfaction. But this does not mean that the economic approach cannot be applied to certain aspects of life, at certain moments in history. Once a particular set of human ends has been, so to speak, leveled—rendered commensurable with each other—it becomes open to analysis in terms of costs and benefits. This is precisely what happened in the late eighteenth century, in the process described by Karl Polanyi as "the great transformation." Land, labor, and capital were stripped of their traditional symbolic value and became visible as many factors of production. There was nothing natural or inevitable about this development; it was the product of a revolutionary change whose roots lay in the social and political history of Europe.

This comes back to a point made by John Kay earlier about the difference between economic and anthropological understandings of human society. Anthropologists might see economic rationality emerging out of certain cultural norms, but they would not try to analyze those cultural norms themselves in terms of economic rationality; they would see them as bedrock, whereas I think the economists would try to analyze the cultural norms themselves in terms of some underlying, implicit rationality. So for the economists the rationality goes all the way down, whereas for the anthropologist or the sociologist it does not. That is a fundamental difference of approach to human society.

In recent decades this process of leveling, as I have called it, has extended beyond the monetary economy into the previously sacrosanct spheres of morality and culture. This is the development I referred to earlier as the triumph of the therapeutic. The collapse of institutional authority, in the first case religious, but also secular, has stripped moral norms of their previous categorical force, but not their power to cause pleasure and pain. So morality has come to be viewed instrumentally as something to be cultivated for its resources of meaning, or else shrugged off as a source of guilt. Feelings such as shame and pride now stand on a level with the old material incentives and can be thrown into the scales alongside them. Becker and other rational choice theorists have simply put a theoretical gloss upon this historical development.

Evidence of the triumph of the therapeutic is all around us. Objects and practices that were previously considered good in themselves are now extolled for their psychic benefits; religion gives us meaning, marriage is good for health, classical music helps us to relax after a stressful day at work, and so forth. This is the ubiquitous language of advertising. But I would like to focus on the meaning of a couple of key terms: guilt and happiness—both of them prominent in modern economic theory—because they reflect this therapeutic shift in our culture particularly clearly.

I will start with guilt. Guilt in the original sense is a legal term, signifying the state of being guilty. Guilt exists whether the guilty individual has any consciousness of it or not. It is not a psychological category. However, over the past hundred years, the meaning of the term has undergone a radical shift. Guilt now primarily signifies a *feeling* of being in the wrong, whether or not this feeling has any basis in fact. It is in this sense that the notion of guilt features in a lot of modern economic theory. For example, according to Becker, guilt is the psychic penalty that we exact on individuals whose behavior we wish to curtail; it is a kind of internalized fine.

This analysis may be appropriate to certain modern societies that have undergone the therapeutic shift, but as a general theory of guilt it must be false. It would have made no sense, for instance, for a tenth-century Chinese to think of his moral debt to his parents as something imposed by them in order to secure their welfare in old age, as Gary Becker analyzes it. For the Chinese youth, and for his parents, it was simply a fact about the moral world, as real as any financial debt. The fact that many modern Chinese *do* think of family relations along the lines suggested by Becker is simply evidence that Confucian norms have lost something of their binding force, and now function in an essentially manipulative fashion.

What I'm assuming here is a fundamental point about the nature of social explanation, which Richard Bronk mentions, and that is the fact that when we interpret a certain human society, the terms in which we interpret it have to build upon the terms in which it interprets itself. This is what distinguishes human sciences from the natural sciences; we are dealing with agents who act according to a certain conception of themselves as thinking and feeling individuals, not as rocks or billiard balls. But I think, perhaps, a lot of economists would not accept that basic premise.

Happiness has undergone a shift in meaning parallel to guilt, although the process started much earlier. For the ancient Greeks happiness, or eudaimonia, was not primarily a state of mind, but a condition of being, comprising such tangible goods as health, wealth, and honor. The English word "happiness" originally had a similar meaning; "We few, we happy few," says Shakespeare's

Henry V to his troops before Agincourt, presumably not with the implication that they are about to enjoy agreeable states of mind!

Yet, by the time of Bentham, happiness had acquired its modern meaning of a subjective mental state, measurable along a single dimension, with only external, causal relations to its objective conditions. So happiness became ripe for economic treatment. All that was lacking was an objective metric. But recent discoveries of a correlation between reported happiness and certain kinds of brain activity have made good the deficiency. The economics of happiness now claims to stand on a firm scientific foundation.

Let me be clear: I have no quarrel with the goal of putting happiness, as opposed to GDP growth, at the center of government policy. I have a lot of sympathy with that goal. My quarrel is with the conception of happiness involved. The problem with it is brought out nicely by these thought experiments involving drugs or virtual reality machines. It might be possible, by means of such artificial devices, to provide a person with a continual stream of pleasant experiences. But that person would not be "happy" in the sense understood by Aristotle or Shakespeare, or anyone prior to the eighteenth century. This view of happiness severs its link with truth and with the human good. Happiness in this sense cannot be a goal of government policy, unless we wish to hand ourselves over to the engineers of *Brave New World*. There has been a lot of talk recently about the moral crisis of capitalism, and perhaps capitalism is in moral crisis. But it would be a great mistake to go straight from the mindless pursuit of wealth to the mindless pursuit of happiness, understood in this subjectivist sense. What we should be doing is thinking, as philosophers have always thought, about the conditions of the good life.

INDEX